T0018154

Becoming Beatrix

The Life of Beatrix Potter
and the World of Peter Rabbit

AMY M. O'QUINN

CHICAGO
REVIEW
PRESS

PUBLISHER'S NOTE: This book is an independently authored and published work of biography and commentary about the life and work of Beatrix Potter. Some text and images that originated with Beatrix Potter are used in this book pursuant to the Fair Use Doctrine or because they first appeared in works that are now in the public domain. This book is not endorsed by or affiliated in any way with any owner of trademarks based on phrases and images that also appear in the works of Beatrix Potter now in the public domain.

The Library of Congress has cataloged the hardcover edition as follows:
Names: O'Quinn, Amy M., author.
Title: Becoming Beatrix : the life of Beatrix Potter and the world of Peter
    Rabbit / Amy M. O'Quinn.
Description: Chicago, Illinois : Chicago Review Press, [2022] | Includes
    bibliographical references and index. | Audience: Ages 8-12. | Audience:
    Grades 4-6. | Summary: "Becoming Beatrix: The Life of Beatrix Potter and
    the World of Peter Rabbit covers Potter's early life and influences,
    artistic work, fascination with animals and the natural sciences, and
    interest and research with fungi, as well as her writing and
    illustration journey and her later years as a wife, farmer,
    businesswoman, environmentalist, and conservationist"— Provided by
    publisher.
Identifiers: LCCN 2021043486 | ISBN 9781641604406 (cloth) | ISBN
    9781641604420 (mobi) | ISBN 9781641604413 (pdf) | ISBN 9781641604437
    (epub)
Subjects: LCSH: Potter, Beatrix, 1866-1943—Juvenile literature. | Authors,
    English—20th century—Biography—Juvenile litera[Bture. | Artists—Great
    Britain—Biography—Juvenile literature. | BISAC: JUVENILE NONFICTION /
    Biography & Autobiography / Literary | JUVENILE NONFICTION / Science &
    Nature / Environmental Conservation & Protection | LCGFT: Biography.
Classification: LCC PR6031.O72 Z82 2022 | DDC 823/.912]—dc23
LC record available at https://lccn.loc.gov/2021043486

Cover design: Preston Pisellini
Cover images: Young Beatrix, The Beatrix Potter Society,
    www.beatrixpottersociety.org.uk
Interior design: Sarah Olson
Interior illustrations: HelloPAPER/Creativemarket.com

Printed in the United States of America

For my mother and sister, Betty McIntyre and
Mindy McHugh—fellow Anglophiles, sheep
lovers, and travel companions.

And for my father, Edward McIntyre,
lifelong agriculturalist and gardener—
just like Beatrix.

CONTENTS

Author's Note

When Beatrix Potter was born in 1866, the Industrial Revolution had already changed the world in a big way. There were major advances in the fields of technology, industry, travel, and communication, and cities like London were growing rapidly as more people moved from rural to urban areas. Even so, much of English society still followed firm rules and had very definite ideas about how homes should be managed and how children should behave.

At the time of Beatrix's birth, Queen Victoria had already been on the throne for more than 28 years. The period during her reign was called the Victorian era, and although the queen modeled and encouraged strong family values and good morals, life then was much different than it is today. Babies or children from wealthy families like Beatrix's often had a hired nurse who took care of them until they were old enough to attend school or have a tutor or governess.

These youngsters might live in nursery rooms on an upper floor of the home and perhaps only saw their parents once or twice a day. They ate their meals in the nursery rather than in the dining room with their parents, at least until they were older. They played with their toys, looked at picture books, took walks with their nannies in the neighborhood, wore nice clothes, and were admonished to stay clean and to act prim and proper. They were expected to be seen but not heard. No one during the Victorian era considered these practices unusual.

Young Beatrix's upbringing was probably no different from that of other privileged children of her day. She was often lonely, with only her younger brother Bertram as a playmate. She also had a complicated relationship with her mother and sometimes felt "hemmed in" by the things she was (or wasn't) expected to do as a girl or young lady in Victorian times—like marrying an acceptable wealthy husband when she was old enough.

Some earlier biographers considered Beatrix's childhood to be too harsh, but it's just the way things were done during that era. However, Beatrix was surrounded by a rich learning environment, and she was able to keep a menagerie of pets (although sometimes secretly), travel extensively with her family, and enjoy many hobbies, such as painting, nature study, and visiting beautiful museums.

It's important keep historical context in mind when reading about Beatrix's life—and about the amazing things she was able to accomplish.

Beatrix Potter Commemorative Coin. *Image used by permission of author*

INTRODUCTION

Thousands of visitors walk up the Brathay slate path to visit Beatrix Potter's Hill Top Farm in the English Lake District region each year. After touring the house, they usually spend time in the old-fashioned garden, viewing the wooden beehive box in the bee bole, admiring the garden gates and doors, vegetable beds, and beautiful heirloom plants and flowers. If they look toward the front pasture, they will probably see Herdwick sheep frisking about.

Occasionally, a guest may catch a glimpse of a rabbit resting beneath a rhubarb plant or hopping near the slate garden wall. Could it be Peter Rabbit trying to sneak past Mr. McGregor to get to the gate? Or is it Benjamin Bunny trying to help his naughty cousin retrieve his little blue coat and slippers left behind during an earlier adventure?

Of course, both bunnies were fictional critters created by Beatrix Potter, although they were based on her real childhood pets. Many of the other beloved characters in her books also had their beginnings from real pets, but of course, those animals didn't wear bonnets or tiny jackets or talk or run their own businesses! Regardless, it's fun to imagine Beatrix's whimsical characters rushing to and fro around Lake District villages tending to the tasks of daily life.

In reality, Beatrix's life story is just as fascinating as the stories of any of her fictional characters. She was born at a time when children were supposed to be seen rather than heard. However, she found much joy in her pets, the natural world, and her art, and her early childhood days in the nursery at 2 Bolton Gardens in London shaped the rest of her life.

It's true that Beatrix was a talented writer and artist, but she was so much more than an illustrator of animals wearing tiny coats, caps, boots, or bonnets. She was also a remarkable scientist, naturalist, conservationist, and sheep farmer.

This is the tale of Beatrix Potter—beyond the bunnies.

Beginnings at
2 Bolton Gardens

"My brother and I were born in London because my father was a lawyer there. But our descent—our interests and our joy was in the north country."

—Beatrix Potter

Beatrix Potter's own real-life story began on Saturday, July 28, 1866, at 2 Bolton Gardens in London's Kensington district. The short, formal birth announcement followed two days later in the *Times* newspaper. Her parents, Rupert and Helen Leech Potter, were both from well-to-do families—so, of course, the arrival of their newborn daughter, Helen Beatrix, merited at least a small mention in Britain's oldest national daily newspaper.

Beatrix's family was not originally from London, however, and they certainly weren't from old money either. In fact, her parents were born and raised in Lancashire, a county in northwest England. Rupert was born in 1833 and Helen in 1839. Both of Beatrix's grandfathers started out as part of the working class, yet they'd eventually made large fortunes from scratch through sheer stubbornness and determination—traits Beatrix herself had plenty of as well.

After many setbacks and even bankruptcy, Beatrix's paternal grandfather, Edmund Potter, had founded Edmund Potter and Co., the largest calico (a brightly colored cotton fabric) printing mill in the world. He was also elected to British Parliament and served as the Liberal representative from Carlisle for 12 years. By all accounts, he was a very successful and influential man. He was married to Jessy Crompton Potter, a famous and feisty beauty in her younger days and the grandmother Beatrix was closest to.

Beatrix's maternal grandfather, John Leech, became a prosperous cotton merchant and owned a sizable and successful mercantile business. He built a large fleet of ships that sailed around the globe, and his name was known all over the world. He was married to Jane Ashton Leech, and Beatrix had fond memories of visiting Gorse Hall, her grandparents' home in northwest England, and their second home in London.

Rupert and Helen, who married in 1863, both inherited great wealth from their parents and had the means to live a lavish lifestyle. To be fair, Rupert had studied law in college and worked hard to qualify as a barrister, or lawyer, in 1857. He did have a law practice in London, but he didn't necessarily have to work to earn an income because he already had plenty of money. He was also very enthusiastic about pursuing the hobby

The view from 2 Bolton Gardens, photographed by Rupert Potter, 1907. © *Victoria and Albert Museum, London*

of photography, which was a relatively new art, and he enjoyed spending a lot of time at one of his exclusive, intellectual London clubs while Helen oversaw their home and paid social calls.

The Potters bought a beautiful four-story home at Bolton Gardens, a new development in rural Kensington, the year before Beatrix was born. Across the street from the house was a small private "pocket park," or small garden, to which only the local residents were given a key to its iron gate. Of course, Rupert and Helen had to pay for the privilege of using the park, but having access to a bit of country in the city was an absolute must for affluent families during those days.

Indeed, 2 Bolton Gardens was a fashionable address for a young, up-and-coming, wealthy couple like the Potters—and Helen definitely wanted to be part of London's elite crowd. Unfortunately, this was a group that often looked down on those whose "new" money came from work and industry in recent generations, so Helen, and sometimes Rupert, downplayed their family ties to the textile regions of northern England. Beatrix, however, was always quite proud of her family's origin and humble roots, calling her ancestors "obstinate, hard headed, *matter of fact* folk."

When their daughter was born, the Potters hired a nurse from the Scottish Highlands named Ann McKenzie to

Beatrix with her parents, Rupert and Helen Potter. *Science History Images / Alamy Stock Photo*

take charge of the third-floor nursery and baby Beatrix. Nurse McKenzie might have had a gloomy disposition, but in addition to basic baby care, she sang songs and read books to her small charge.

Nurse McKenzie took Beatrix for daily walks in the parks near Bolton Gardens, introduced her to the wonders of nature, and encouraged her to draw and paint, as the little girl showed artistic talent from a very early age. The nurse also filled Beatrix's head with fanciful fairy stories and Scottish folklore. Ann McKenzie's influence during Beatrix's early years definitely shaped her imagination, how she viewed the world around her, and the whimsical stories she would later create.

Like most wealthy parents of the Victorian era, Helen and Rupert pretty much left the day-to-day upbringing of their child to the nurse. They might occasionally visit the nursery, but usually Nurse McKenzie would present a sweet-smelling, nicely dressed little Beatrix to her parents for a short visit downstairs once or twice a day. But Rupert, especially, encouraged Beatrix's love of art, science, natural history, and literature and made sure her nursery was a rich learning environment. Beatrix always had a warm relationship with her father and shared many of his interests.

Beatrix later claimed that she could recall memories from her earliest childhood. "I can remember quite plainly from one to two years old; not only facts, like learning to walk but places and sentiments—the way things impressed a very young child."

She certainly remembered Camfield Place, the home her paternal grandparents, Edmund and Jessy Crompton Potter, bought in Hertfordshire in 1866 after Edmund retired from Parliament. Camfield Place was within easy traveling distance from London, and Beatrix's family visited often. Later, she wrote that it was "the

Children in Victorian London

Children from wealthy families like Beatrix's might've had very little interaction with their parents, but at least they lived in safe, comfortable homes. They had plenty of food, soft beds, and probably books and toys. They were given lessons at home or sent to school to learn. If they got sick, a doctor would visit their home and treat them, although healthcare was not as reliable as it is today.

Other children in Victorian London, however, were not so fortunate. Sadly, many boys and girls were forced to work long hours in factories, shipyards, or mines. Some little boys were chimney sweeps, and often girls went into domestic service as a kitchen helper or maid when they were very young. Some children's work was unsafe and the conditions were unhealthy. Often, the children were treated very badly—and most had no opportunity to get an education.

Some children were orphans and lived on the streets with no one to take care of them. They relied on handouts from passersby, or even stole food to keep from starving. Some resorted to a life of crime. There were some charities and organizations that

(continued on next page)

(continued from previous page)

tried to help the children, but there were too many youngsters who needed assistance, and conditions were dire.

Finally, the Factory and Workshop Act of 1878 banned work for children younger than 10, and writers, like Charles Dickens, also brought the plight of poor children to the public, raising awareness of the terrible situation. In addition, in 1891, the Society for the Prevention of Cruelty to Children was established, and child welfare in London slowly began to improve.

place I love best in the world" with "the sweet balmy air where I have been so happy as a child." She thought it was almost perfect—from "the notes of the stable clock and the all pervading smell of new-mown hay" to "the distant sounds of the farmyard."

Of Camfield Place, she also recorded, "There was something rapturous to us London children in the unlimited supply of new milk. I remember always the first teas of the visit when we were thirsty and tired. How I watched at the window for the little farm-boy, staggering along the carriage-drive with the cans! It came up warm in a great snuff-coloured [sic] jug which seemed to have no bottom, and made the milk look blue."

During Beatrix's early years, she was also introduced to another special place. Grandfather Potter was an avid fisherman and had begun the tradition of renting a summer holiday house in the Scottish countryside near Perthshire. The home was on the River Tay, the longest river in Scotland. Beatrix's father, Rupert, especially looked forward to the family trip each summer because he also enjoyed hunting and fishing like his father.

Rupert continued the tradition of renting Scottish vacation homes for his own growing family. Then, in 1871, when Beatrix had just turned five, he found and leased the perfect summer getaway near Dunkeld, Scotland's historic cathedral city. Dalguise House was on the western shore of the River Tay where the fishing was excellent. Rupert always invited family and special friends to visit at Dalguise House and spent a lot of time photographing his patient, good-natured guests in the beautiful surroundings.

The Potters stayed at Dalguise House every summer for the next 10 years. The Scottish landscape provided a feast for Beatrix's eyes, nourishment for her imagination, and freedom for her spirit. It was this landscape she would compare all others to. She loved it from her very first visit. As an adult, she claimed that some of her happiest childhood moments were spent at Dalguise House.

During the summer holidays in Scotland, Beatrix had more freedom than she was given in London. She explored. She played with her pets and investigated the natural world. She walked among the flowers and plants and also observed wildlife. She sketched, drew, and recorded everything she saw to her heart's content. Her creativity and fancies were given full reign.

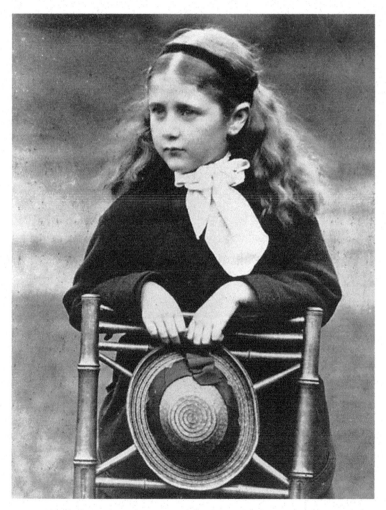

Beatrix at about the age of five. *The Beatrix Potter Society, www .beatrixpottersociety.org.uk*

"Everything was romantic in my imagination. The woods were peopled by the mysterious good folk. The Lords and Ladies of the last century walked with me along the overgrown paths, and picked the old-fashioned flowers among the box and rose hedges of the garden . . . I lived in a separate world."

In a biographical entry for *The Horn Book* years later, Beatrix also noted, "So it sometimes happens that the town child is more alive to the fresh beauty of the country than a child who is country born."

Beatrix definitely felt more alive in the countryside, as she never really liked city living nor her home at 2 Bolton Gardens. Dalguise House became "home to her heart." It was also in this area where the story seeds for Peter Rabbit would be planted years later.

Beatrix was seldom allowed to play with other children, as her mother feared they might be the source of germs, or perhaps a bad influence. Beatrix was often sick when she was young, so maybe her mother believed she was keeping her daughter from being exposed to more serious illnesses. In any case, Beatrix's early days were quite solitary, with only her nurse as a companion.

When she was almost six, however, Beatrix got a full-time playmate—a baby brother. She finally had someone who would eventually share her many interests, activities, and an ever-growing menagerie of pets.

Beatrix with her younger brother Bertram at Dalguise House in Scotland. *The Beatrix Potter Society, www.beatrixpottersociety .org.uk*

Walter Bertram Potter was born on March 14, 1872, and immediately joined his older sister and Nurse McKenzie in the third-floor nursery.

Beatrix was thrilled with her new sibling from the first day, and the two would remain close all their lives. Both children went by their middle names, and they were known to family and close friends as B and Bertie. Nurse McKenzie naturally spent more time caring for baby Bertram, so a governess named Florrie Hammond was hired for Beatrix. Miss Hamond, who would stay with the Potters until 1883 when Beatrix was almost 17 years old, was another person who helped shape the girl's life. It was a common practice for young ladies of wealthy Victorian families to be educated at home, and Miss Hammond did a good job. She taught Beatrix the basic subjects of reading, writing, and arithmetic, but she also tried to incorporate her young student's interests into the curriculum. There was a lot of nature study and plenty of time for painting and drawing.

Beatrix also enjoyed picture books. At that time, children's book illustration was considered high art, and children's books became part of Victorian fashion, like architecture and home decor. Well-to-do parents took delight in buying artistic books for their offspring, and Rupert was no exception. Beatrix spent hours looking at the illustrations of Walter Crane, Kate Greenaway, Randolph Caldecott, and Edward Lear, artists whose creative styles definitely influenced Beatrix's tastes.

As for reading, Beatrix had a wide variety of interests. When she was very young, she "liked [to hear] silly stories about other little girls' doings"—and "goody goody, powder-in-the-jam" books. According to historian Linda

Lear, Beatrix would've almost certainly been exposed to the popular children's books written by Anna Barbauld, including *Little Stories for Little Children* and *Hymns in Prose for Children*. These books were very small and designed to be held by children's tiny hands. When she became an author, Beatrix insisted that her books should be small too.

When she was six or seven, Beatrix was also given a copy of Lewis Carroll's *Alice's Adventures in Wonderland*. She wasn't as interested in the story as much as she was enthralled by the delightful illustrations by John Tenniel. In fact, she tried creating her own illustrations for *Alice* and other favorite books. These early attempts at re-creating favorite drawings helped her develop her skills and refine her own whimsical drawing style.

Looking at photographs of Beatrix when she was a little girl, it's obvious that Victorian book illustrations must have also influenced children's clothing styles. She was a very pretty child and could have easily stepped right out of one of her storybooks.

Later, she wrote, "Of course, what I wore was absurdly uncomfortable; white piqué starched frocks just like Tenniel's 'Alice in Wonderland,' and cotton stockings striped round and round like a zebra's legs."

Of her headbands, she said, "mine used to be black velvet on Sundays, and either black or brown ribbon week days. I remember the bands fastened with a bit of elastic, looped over a button behind the ear; it hurt."

Beatrix's family was part of the Unitarian church and attended services at one of the Unitarian chapels in London each Sunday. Most of Rupert's and Helen's friends were of the same denomination, and many of those friendships had been formed during their childhood years in Lancashire.

The Potters were especially close to William Gaskell, a Unitarian minister, and his wife, Elizabeth, one of the most well-known British novelists of the time. In fact, Gaskell, who had also been close to Beatrix's grandfather Edmund, usually visited the Potters during their Scottish vacations, especially after his wife died at a relatively young age. Beatrix was extremely fond of the elderly gentleman and counted him a very special friend.

Unitarians during this time were known as "dissenters" or "nonconformists" because they were Protestants who disagreed with, and refused to follow, the doctrines and traditions of the Church of England, also known as the Anglican Church. Many Unitarians were well-educated and wealthy, however, and most were very concerned with social justice and reform.

Regardless of Helen's desire to move in the best social circles, the Unitarian community was fairly small and rather isolated from other groups. This limited the number of people the Potters, including Beatrix, interacted

Beatrix with her dear friend William Gaskell in Scotland.
© *Victoria and Albert Museum, London*

with. Moreover, Rupert's personal theological views meant the Potters usually didn't attend holiday celebrations or gatherings—or exchange gifts.

Beatrix, who was full of imagination and delight in the fanciful, longed to participate in the traditional church festivals and holidays. It would've also given her the opportunity to play with other children during the most magical time of year. But in the Potter household, Christmas was a day that was acknowledged rather than celebrated. Of course, Beatrix was probably disappointed that she couldn't join in the merriment and fun of the season.

Yet despite her lack of happy holiday memories, Beatrix always loved festive occasions—and some of her later illustrations were of bunnies frolicking about and celebrating during the Christmas season. She channeled her early disappointments into painting warm, cozy scenes that would delight audiences for years to come. She found a way to re-create the joy of Christmas that she had missed as a child.

GIRLHOOD AND
GROWING UP

---

*"I do not remember a time when I did not try to invent
pictures and make for myself a fairyland amongst the
wild flowers, the animals, fungi, mosses, woods and
streams, all the thousand objects of the countryside."*

—BEATRIX POTTER

Beatrix was always happy to get away from London,
so she looked forward to the family's summer vacations in Scotland. And fortunately for Beatrix, the Potters
also took an additional two-week trip away from home
each spring. London was called the Big Smoke because of
all the smoke pollution from the large number of factories and industries in the city. Soot was always a big problem, even inside houses since they were usually heated

with coal-burning stoves. The Potters' beautiful home at 2 Bolton Gardens was no exception.

Rupert and Helen depended on their many servants to clean everything from top to bottom in their London home while the family enjoyed their short vacation at the seaside or some other pleasant destination, where the air was fresh and clean. The Potters often visited resort towns on the southern English coast, such as Ilfracombe, Minehead, Falmouth, or Sidmouth. But no matter where she went, Beatrix was fascinated by the beauty of the natural world around her.

Like her parents, Beatrix was in the habit of carrying around a sketchbook to draw and record what she saw. In fact, both her mother and father were artistic, and Helen had created several pretty watercolor paintings before she was married. Rupert leaned more toward sketching and drawing caricatures, and in fact, one of his college sketchbooks contains a playful illustration of a flying duck wearing a bonnet. Beatrix probably saw her father's sketchbooks when she was young, and perhaps remembered this drawing when she created the unforgettable Jemima Puddle-Duck.

Beatrix's earliest sketchbooks show that she was already an accomplished artist by the time she turned nine. In one sketchbook labeled DALGUISE 1875, she drew caterpillars and wrote descriptions of butterflies and birds' eggs that are quite impressive and detailed for one so young. A year later she was drawing rabbits wearing colorful clothing—sledding, ice skating, and holding an

umbrella on a blustery day. Beatrix obviously had a keen
sense of humor, even as a little girl.

Beatrix loved animals and had countless pets growing
up. Like many other children, she had dogs, including
the much-loved Sandy, a brown Scotch terrier who came
from Dalguise, and later Spot, a springer spaniel. Spot
often traveled with the family in carriages or on trains,
and apparently he had a winning personality. He had to
be "hoisted on to the top of the railway bus in front of
the luggage. He smiled benignly between his curls and
usually captivated the driver."

But Spot was also notorious for trying to take rides
without the Potters! According to Beatrix, "The difficulty was to prevent his riding off in omnibuses, like any
other gentleman."

Beatrix and Bertram, however, had many other
unusual pets as well. In fact, the nursery at 2 Bolton Gardens was a zoo at times, and the Potter parents were not
always aware of the menagerie of pets living on the third
floor of their home. Over the years, the children had
mice, salamanders, water newts, lizards, frogs (including a green one named Punch), bats, a canary, a family of
snails, a tortoise, a wild duck, a ring snake, birds, guinea
pigs, and of course, rabbits.

Despite the children's best care and efforts, sometimes the animals escaped. On one occasion, Beatrix

recorded, "Sally (the snake) and four black newts escaped overnight. Caught one black newt in the school room and another in the larder, but nothing seen of poor Sally, who is probably sporting outside somewhere."

Although the Potter children loved their pets, they were rather matter of fact when the animals died. They'd had enough science lessons and visits to natural history museums and their grandparents' farm to understand the cycle of life. Moreover, like many people of the Victorian era, they were very interested in studying animal anatomy and learning the art of taxidermy. It wasn't unusual for Beatrix and Bertram to skin a dead animal or boil down a carcass to obtain the skeleton for studying, notetaking, measuring, comparing, or sketching. Of course, this practice may seem strange to us now, but it was common among self-taught naturalists and even some artists at that time.

In November 1878, at Miss Hammond's recommendation, 13-year-old Beatrix began taking drawing lessons with Miss Cameron. The lessons lasted until May 1883, and Beatrix learned "freehand, model, geometry, perspective, and a little water-colour flower painting."

The student, however, didn't always agree with the teacher. Beatrix had already developed her own style, and reasoned, "Painting is an awkward thing to teach, except the details of the medium. If you and your master

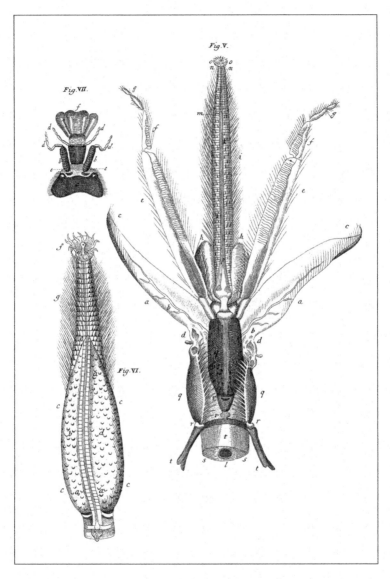

Victorian Nature Study Drawing: Mouth parts of a honeybee and wasp. *Wellcome Collection. Attribution 4.0 International (CC BY 4.0)*

are determined to look at nature and art in two different directions you are sure to stick."

Later, she had additional lessons with Mrs. A, but again, Beatrix wrestled with the idea of being told how to draw or paint. The lessons were expensive, and Mrs. A required her students to use oil paints while Beatrix preferred watercolors. Beatrix didn't want to waste her father's money or the opportunity, so she gamely went along with what she was asked to do in class. But she also stated, "Of course, I shall paint just as I like when not with her." Unsurprisingly, the lessons didn't last very long.

Beatrix's world wasn't large. She spent the majority of her time at home or at parks and museums close to Bolton Gardens in the company of Bertram and Miss Hammond. Many of her sketches from that time are scenes of everyday places and ordinary items. She also continued trying to imitate the illustrations in books drawn by her favorite artists.

In truth, Beatrix couldn't help herself. She *had* to draw! Later, she wrote, "It is all the same, drawing, painting, modelling [sic], the irresistible desire to copy any beautiful object which strikes the eye. Why cannot one be content to look at it? I cannot rest, I must draw, however poor the result."

Sometimes Beatrix found those "beautiful objects" in the most unexpected places. In fact, once when her family was attending a small dinner, she began painting the pineapple that was to be served to the guests.

She hurried to finish and completed the painting just as the pineapple was being cut. How frustrating for the artist!

She noted, "I felt fit to kick under my chair. I thought there would be none left."

The next year, she recorded, "in the middle of September, I caught myself in the back yard making a careful and admiring copy of the swill bucket [container for food scraps, often saved for pigs], and the laugh it gave me brought me around."

As she became more skilled, Beatrix relied less on copying her favorite artists' illustrations to learn technique. She began to *create* sketches and paintings from her own imagination. Of course, she still used her animals as subject matter, and by 1880, she was making a serious study of rabbits and how they looked in various positions. Later on, these keen observations would be extremely valuable to Beatrix's work.

Rupert had many interesting friends and contacts, including the wildly successful Pre-Raphaelite artist Sir John Everett Millais. Millais was part of a group of painters who called themselves the Pre-Raphaelite Brotherhood. The group's name was meant to show its members' displeasure and opposition to the Royal Academy of Arts promoting the works of the great art master, Raphael, a Renaissance painter who used dramatic strokes and color to depict classical ideals. The Pre-Raphaelites believed that artists should portray only "serious" matters and subjects they knew, such as nature, and use the most realistic style possible.

In addition to his other celebrated works, Millais also painted portraits of some of England's most famous citizens and statesmen, including William Gladstone, who was serving his last year as Britain's prime minister.

Millais often asked Rupert to take photographs of backgrounds or the people he was painting so he would have something to reference when the sitters were not present. Beatrix sometimes accompanied her father when he visited Millais's studio, and she enjoyed learning how an artist lived and worked. He even took time to show the young girl how to mix paints.

Beatrix was very shy, and Millais enjoyed teasing her just to see her blush—but he also realized that she had great artistic talent and encouraged her. The renowned artist paid her a high compliment by stating that "plenty of people can *draw*, but you and my son John have observation."

Beatrix also enjoyed accompanying her father to art shows and galleries, and she was quite definite in her opinions on the works she saw there. She became a knowledgeable art critic while observing some of the greatest art masterpieces in the world.

"I never thought there *could* be such pictures. It is almost too much to see them all at once—just fancy seeing five magnificent Van Dyck's side by side, before *me*

Sir John Everett Millais. Photograph by John & Chas. Watkins. *Wellcome Collection. Attribution 4.0 International (CC BY 4.0)*

Beatrix and the Old Masters

Beatrix enjoyed visiting museums and art galleries with her father to study great paintings of her own time and those of the Old Masters. This title referred to skilled and often famous European painters who usually lived before 1830. The paintings of the Old Masters are worth a great deal of money and displayed in highly secured areas in museums.

There were different groups of Old Masters, depending on the years in which they lived and created art, including Renaissance, Baroque, Dutch, Rococo, Neoclassism, and Romanticism. Beatrix became quite an informed art critic, and she recorded her thoughts and impressions in her journal. She listed many of her favorite artists and why she liked them. She also listed the ones she did not like—and why!

Beatrix's artistic style would differ from the paintings of the Old Masters she studied and discussed as a girl and young woman. However, the knowledge she gained during these years was very important in her development as an artist and illustrator.

who never thought to see one. It is rather a painful pleasure, but I have seldom felt such a great one."

Beatrix also began to express her artistic independence when she disagreed with her father's statement that
he didn't like a particular painting because he couldn't
understand it. She wrote, "I had rather a picture I can't
understand than one with nothing to be understood."

Her favorite artists included Millais, especially his
painting *Ophelia*, and landscape artist J. M. W. Turner.
But Beatrix was also impressed with the work of other
female artists and "took particular note of their subject
matter and their drawing technique." These included
Angelica Kauffmann, Lady Louisa Waterford, and Rosa
Bonheur. Beatrix was obviously motivated by what she
saw and inspired to continue improving her own skills,
because she declared, "I *will* do something sooner or
later."

Beatrix kept a journal or diary from 1880 or 1881 until
1897, when she was 30 years old, but it was no ordinary diary. It was written in secret code. Perhaps Beatrix
was trying to keep her mother's prying eyes from seeing
what she was writing, but she developed her own special cipher for recording her thoughts, feelings, current
events, political news, and observations.

The code contained some numbers and a few sym-
bols, but mostly it was a substitution of letter for letter.

Beatrix became so fluent with her invented code that she was able to write long, unbroken passages quickly in progressively tinier print. Sometimes she used lined exercise books, and at other times she wrote on mismatched scraps of paper that were later sewn together to form a booklet of sorts.

Apparently, Beatrix never spoke about her journal to anyone else, but in a letter written to a cousin a few weeks before her death in 1943, she recalled, "I used to write long-winded descriptions, hymns (!) and records of conversations in a kind of cypher shorthand, which I am now unable to read even with a magnifying glass."

Beatrix never considered that anyone other than herself would ever read her entries, and she didn't write every day. A relative found the parts of her journal in her home after her death, but it just looked like a jumble of books and papers in cipher writing. Eventually, it was all given to the Britain's National Trust for safekeeping.

Thankfully, some of the papers were loaned to Potter scholar and specialist Leslie Linder in 1953 to see if he could solve the mystery. Beatrix had complicated the task because she didn't always distinguish capital letters from lowercase letters, nor did she indicate where one paragraph ended and another began. It was all continuous script, and the later entries were almost too small to read.

It took Linder five years, but he finally broke the code in 1958 and was able to transcribe the journal's 200,000 words. It is believed that Beatrix probably destroyed some of her earliest entries when she was older, thinking them unworthy to keep. Therefore, it's possible that the original journal could've been much longer.

Very little was known about Beatrix's life during the years she kept her journal, so Leslie Linder's patience and determination revealed a treasure trove of information about what happened in her teens and twenties. It also gave a more complete picture of the young woman's hopes, dreams, struggles, and desires.

In 1882, Rupert Potter decided not to lease Dalguise House for the summer, "probably stopped by the ridiculous rent," and had to find something else. At first Beatrix was disappointed, as she loved both Scotland and Dalguise House, and looked forward to going there each year. She wouldn't be sad for long, however. Her father chose to lease Wray Castle in the English Lake District, and Beatrix's life was about to change. She was being introduced to the land that she would come to claim as her own, and the place with which her name would forever be associated.

The Potters arrived at Wray Castle in the county of Cumbria on July 21, 1882. The house was built in 1845 by Dr. James Dawson, a retired Liverpool surgeon, and designed to look like a medieval Norman castle, complete with rounded, crenellated turrets and arrow slits in the walls. (Historically, a *crenellated* turret or wall had gaps at the top through which a castle's defenders could shoot arrows or fire ammunition at the enemy.) Wray Castle is situated on the west side of Lake Windermere and took seven years to complete.

From the very beginning, Beatrix was delighted by the beautiful landscape—the tarns (ponds), becks (streams), and fells (high hills or mountains). She and Bertram freely explored the countryside, rowed boats on the lake, and took walks to some of the villages nearby.

Wray Castle in Cumbria, England. *Wikimedia Commons/Drangob*

"Went to Hawkshead on the 19th. Had a series of adventures. Inquired the way three times, lost continually, alarmed by collies at every farm, stuck in stiles, chased once by cows."

It's also possible that Beatrix visited Near Sawrey during that time, the village where she would one day live, since it was also near Wray Castle. The Potters took a drive around nearby Esthwaite Water that summer with their special guest John Bright, one of Britain's greatest public speakers. So, according to Potter biographer Linda Lear, the family would've certainly passed through the tiny hamlet on their way around the lake.

As usual, the Potters hosted other family and friends at their summer home as well. They also met the local vicar, or preacher, named Hardwicke Drummond Rawnsley, a pleasant, intelligent man in his early 30s. Rupert immediately felt a kinship with the young vicar, who also enjoyed photography, poetry, and literature. He'd studied at Oxford and even published a couple of books and many essays. Rawnsley had also traveled extensively and could discuss ideas on many topics. In short, he was a "man of high confidence and tremendous vitality." Unsurprisingly, the vicar, along with his wife Edith and son Noel, were the Potters' frequent guests.

Rawnsley also immediately recognized another kindred spirit in Beatrix. He noticed her drawing and painting and knew she loved natural history and being outdoors. They discussed geology and archeology, subjects they both enjoyed. He also "introduced her to his conviction of the importance of conservation and protection."

The young vicar was passionate about preserving the cultural traditions and land in the Lake District from commercial development. In fact, he would later become one of the founders of Britain's National Trust for Places of Historic Interest or Natural Beauty, or its more common name, the National Trust.

For Beatrix, Hardwicke Rawnsley became a mentor and "someone who loved the things she loved and who was prepared to fight to preserve them." He would be a lifelong friend and a big influence in her life—and give her help and encouragement to pursue her publishing dreams in the years to come.

FEVERS AND FUNGI

"Now of all hopeless things to draw, I should think the very worst is a fine fat fungus." —BEATRIX POTTER

The year 1883 brought more changes for Beatrix. For one, 11-year-old Bertram finished up his schooling at home and prepared to attend boarding school at The Grange in Eastbourne. The siblings had been inseparable for years, enjoying the same hobbies and activities. Beatrix would definitely miss her younger brother.

Then, Miss Hammond stated she'd taught Beatrix all she could and made plans to leave the Potters' household. Beatrix, who was almost 17 and had no other companions or friends her own age, figured she would now concentrate fully on her painting. After all, she would be left at home with only her parents and was done with her schooling—or so she thought.

On April 18, 1883, the day before Bertram left for Eastbourne, Helen made a big announcement: she had employed a new governess to tutor Beatrix in German and Latin and act as a lady's companion. This news didn't go over well with Beatrix, who envisioned the studies "cutting off more and more time for painting." She was very upset with her mother, even though the arrangement was to be short-term. But as a young lady in the Victorian era, Beatrix knew she had no choice in the matter. She controlled her temper and resolutely accepted her mother's plan.

"I thought to have settled down quietly—but it seems it *can not* [sic] be. Only a year, but if it is like the last it will be a lifetime—I can't settle to anything but my painting, I lost my patience over everything else. There is nothing to be done, I must watch things pass."

Beatrix's fears were unfounded. When Miss Annie Carter arrived at the Potter home in September 1883, Beatrix was surprised to meet a friendly young woman who was only three years older than her. Miss Carter also represented a kind of freedom that Beatrix had never experienced. She had lived in Germany, traveled a good bit, and been financially independent for some time.

These were things that Beatrix, dutiful daughter of Rupert and Helen Potter, knew nothing about. Like other wealthy girls, she was expected to either get married or live at home with her parents for the rest of her life. Therefore, hearing about Annie Carter's experiences as an independent woman during Victorian times might have inspired Beatrix to think differently about her own future.

In any case, Miss Carter was pleasant company for the lonely girl, and Beatrix proved she was a good student of languages as she became more fluent in German. To her surprise, she also discovered she enjoyed Latin. Beatrix had dreaded having another governess, but Annie Carter became a treasured friend and would remain so for life. Her family would also play a big part in Beatrix's journey to becoming a published author.

Indeed, Beatrix needed a good friend, as the rest of 1883 and even 1884 brought more sadness. She lost an uncle, her Grandmother Leech, Grandfather Potter, and her beloved friend William Gaskell in less than a year. She wrote of Gaskell, "Dear old man, he has had a very peaceful end. If ever any one [sic] led a blameless peaceful life, it was he. Another old friend gone to rest. How few are left."

During this time, Beatrix also recorded the loss of some her favorite pets in her journal, including Judy, the green lizard who had given "a great deal of pleasure," a group of garden snails known as the Bill family, and Punch, the green frog, which had lived for five or six years and traveled with Beatrix on many of the Potters' journeys. She felt the same when her "happy and affectionate" dormouse, Xarifa, died of old age. Beatrix called her the "sweetest animal I ever knew."

Beatrix always tended to battle depression, but of course, sad events made the feelings worse. It's no surprise that she felt down after the deaths of so many beloved family members and pets. Her unhappiness was apparent in this journal entry: "I wish for many things, and yet how much I have to be thankful for, but these odious fits of low spirits would spoil any life."

Fear of change, which can bother many people, also caused Beatrix stress. Of course, she had been upset when her father chose not to rent Dalguise House in 1882, but when he considered leasing it again in 1884, she was afraid that it would be too changed from the way she had remembered it and ruin her happy memories. She wrote, "I feel an extraordinary dislike to this idea, a childish dislike, but the memory of that home is the only bit of childhood I have left."

Beatrix mourned the end of her childhood days, while perhaps seeing nothing but a long stretch of endless days stuck at 2 Bolton Gardens. She recorded, "the future is dark and uncertain, let me keep the past."

In the end, Rupert chose to rent another place in Edinburgh, Scotland, instead.

Beatrix turned 18 on July 28, 1884, but her feelings on the matter were mixed. She wrote, "I am eighteen today. How time does go. I feel as if I had been going on such a time."

Then, after Bertram returned to boarding school after a visit home in September, he left her "the responsibility of a precious bat. It is a charming little creature, quite tame and apparently happy as long as it has sufficient flies and raw meat."

Perhaps caring for Bertram's bat helped Beatrix's feelings, at least a bit. It does seem as if her animals always brought her comfort during the hard days, as did her art. But Beatrix also worried about her quiet 12-year-old brother and how he might turn out. She loved Bertram dearly and was proud that he was at the top of class, but she must've seen a weakness in his character that concerned her. She wrote, "I wonder how he will turn out? Sometimes I am hopeful, sometimes I am feared. . . . The best upbringing has sometimes failed in this family, and I am afraid Bertram has *it* in him. Heaven grant it is not so, but I am afraid sometimes."

The "it" seems to have been alcoholism, as the addiction was common in the Leech family. In fact, one of Beatrix's uncles died from alcoholism, so perhaps she feared her brother might face the same problem when he got older. Bertram was a sensitive, artistic boy who also struggled with new situations, such as being sent to a different school at his father's insistence, which did not work out. Beatrix's concern was understandable.

Beatrix also faced the worries and trials of being ill. She'd never been a very healthy child and often got sick, but in March 1885 she came down with what was probably rheumatic fever. A lot of her long, beautiful hair fell out, and the rest was cut off, which was a common treatment for fevers.

She wrote, "Now that the sheep is shorn, I may say without pride that I have seldom seen a more beautiful head of hair than mine. Last summer it was very thick and within about four inches of my knees, being more than a yard long."

Beatrix's hair was still quite short, however, when her parents hosted a large party on July 28, 1885, to celebrate her 19th birthday. Nonetheless, she was a very pretty young woman with an oval face, wide-set blue eyes, a slim figure, and good posture.

Beatrix's education with Miss Carter, her "very good-natured and intelligent" governess, also ended that month. Beatrix would miss the companionship, but she was also thrilled for her teacher, who was soon to be married to Edwin Moore, a civil engineer.

She wasn't quite as happy for her beautiful cousin, Kate Potter, who was also getting married. Kate was the daughter of Rupert's oldest brother Crompton, who had passed away in 1883. Beatrix strongly disapproved of her cousin's choice for a husband and wrote, "If this is what beauty leads to, I am well content to have a red nose and a shorn head, I may be lonely, but better that than an unhappy marriage."

Beatrix was relieved to see the end of 1885, but admitted she was "terribly afraid of the future." Unfortunately, the next year and half brought her more sickness and another bout of rheumatic fever, and she suffered great pain in her feet and legs. At one point she reported that she "could not be turned in bed without screaming

Beatrix, Rupert, and Bertram Potter with Spot at Lingholm, a country house in Cumbria, England, 1885. Beatrix had recently had her hair "shorn" due to being ill with rheumatic fever. *The Beatrix Potter Society, www.beatrixpottersociety.org.uk*

out." Ultimately, she was unable to do much but rest and recover, and in June 1887 she wrote, "Amazed to find myself in summer, having last seen the trees in winter. I have had no spring."

During the time she was recuperating, Beatrix found ways to amuse herself. Of course, she read books, sketched, and painted, but she also became interested in using Bertram's microscope to see the fine details of the specimens she was drawing. Some of her watercolor paintings from that time show the full depiction of some insects, with additional sketches of magnified wings, legs, or antennae.

According to biographer Linda Lear, "Such drawings suggest that her observations of the natural world and the relationship between nature and art was becoming more sophisticated."

All the while, Beatrix continued creating colorful illustrations, including those of woodland animals (especially rabbits) and other things such as beautiful Christmas cards and table place cards in 1889. Her uncle, Sir Henry Enfield Roscoe, who was married to Rupert's sister Lucy, was quite impressed with Beatrix's work. Knowing that both Potter children were interested in earning money, he suggested that Beatrix create some card designs to submit, and hopefully sell, to publishers.

By Easter 1890, she had created six card designs featuring "that charming rascal Benjamin Bouncer our tame Jack Hare." Beatrix had bought the large rabbit, also known as Bounce, earlier in the year at a London bird shop, and snuck him home in a paper bag. She used him as a model, and he proved to be a good investment. With Bertram's help, she sent the card designs to five publishers. Only one firm, Hildesheimer & Faulkner, was interested. It sent Beatrix a check for six pounds and asked for more sketches.

The designs were first published as Christmas cards and later in a beautiful booklet of verses written by Frederic E. Weatherly, titled *A Happy Pair*. Only Beatrix's initials, H.B.P., were listed at the bottom of each illustration, but the 24-year-old felt as if her artistic career had finally begun. Moreover, she liked her first taste of financial independence.

Beatrix created more watercolor sketches and sent them to another potential publisher, Frederick Warne & Co. The firm declined because it did not publish booklets, but it stated it liked Beatrix's illustrations and would be happy to consider any future book ideas and drawings.

Although Beatrix was thrilled with her artistic success, she had reason to mourn again. Her favorite grandmother, Jessy Crompton Potter, died in September 1891 in her 90th year. Beatrix was devastated. The two of them had been close, and Beatrix had been very proud of her Crompton roots and feisty ancestors. She had also greatly admired Jessy's beauty, lively personality, and strong character. Moreover, Camfield Place would be sold, taking away another of Beatrix's favorite childhood places. Her life seemed to be in constant change.

Beatrix filled her days as best she could. She especially enjoyed going to see her former governess, Annie Carter Moore, and her new baby boy Noel, who was born on Christmas Eve. Annie went on to have seven more children. They didn't live far from Beatrix, so she visited their happy home often. The children were delighted when Beatrix came, as she often brought along her pets or gifts, and the Moore siblings always held a special place in Beatrix's heart as well.

Years later, they recalled that "she was very pretty . . . with sparkling blue eyes. Her voice was quiet and soft, though slightly higher in pitch than average. When she told of some amusing incident she gave a little twist to her mouth which, combined with a smile, they found quite fascinating."

Yet, much to her mother's dismay, it didn't seem that Beatrix was going to find a husband. Most Victorian-era women married quite young, and Beatrix was already in her mid-20s. Of course, she wasn't opposed to marrying for love, but she had not found the right person—and she was very shy. Moreover, her mother had specific ideas of who the "right person" could be. In any case,

Beatrix with her rabbit, Bounce, on a leash at Heath Park, Birnam, Scotland, in 1892. *WorldPhotos / Alamy Stock Photo*

Beatrix seemed content enough with her animals, art, and family travels.

When the Potters stayed at Heath Park in Birnam, a village near Perth, Scotland, in the summer of 1892, Beatrix was overjoyed. She would be able to spend time with Bertram, who would soon be attending Oxford University. Bounce traveled with the family to Scotland as well, but as a precaution to keep him safe, Beatrix took him out in the garden on a leather strap. Apparently, the sight of a rabbit on a leash amused the staff at Heath Park!

Rupert provided Beatrix with a small cart and pony, and she enjoyed getting out to ride and explore the Scottish countryside each day. She took photographs with her father's old camera and became quite good at it. She sketched and painted, but she also used the opportunity to pursue her latest interest—fungi. Tramping through the woods hunting mushrooms to paint might have seemed a strange thing for a young lady in her 20s to do, but Helen and Rupert had no problem with it. After all, nature study was a very acceptable pastime for wealthy Victorian women.

Beatrix had created some watercolors of mushrooms in 1887, but at first, she simply wanted to capture their beautiful shapes and colors with her paint and brush. She shared her fungi illustrations with Charlie McIntosh, the intelligent, self-taught Scottish naturalist and country postman she'd known since she was a child.

McIntosh was a tall, thin man, and painfully shy. Beatrix once wrote, "I would not make fun of him for worlds, but he reminded me so much of a damaged lamp post." She also realized he knew more about fungi than even the most educated scientists, so she was pleased when McIntosh liked her work and offered to send her more specimens by mail when she returned to London. He kept his word, and Beatrix, wanting to be a good student, began learning the scientific names and classifications of the fungi she was painting.

She had no idea that her interest in fungi would lead to another phase of her creative career, but more changes were just around the corner.

Discoveries, Disregard, and the Road to Recognition

"My dear Noel, I don't know what to write to you, so I shall tell you a story about four little rabbits whose names were Flopsy, Mopsy, Cotton-tail, and Peter." —Beatrix Potter, *in a letter to Noel Moore, September 4, 1893*

The Potters returned to Scotland in 1893 where Rupert rented another house, called Eastwood, on the bank of the Tay River in Dunkeld. It wasn't far from where they had stayed the previous summer, and Beatrix was able to consult Charlie McIntosh again as she continued studying and painting fungi specimens—60 in total, all of which are marked Eastwood, 1893.

In July, Beatrix discovered what she believed to be a rare pine cone fungus and showed it to McIntosh. He thought it was *Strobilomyces strobilaceus,* an extremely rare species nicknamed the "old man of the woods," but sent it to a laboratory to be sure. He was right! In

Strobilomyces strobilaceus, a fungus also known as the "old man of the woods." *Strobilomyces strobilaceus by Andreas Kunze is licensed under CC BY-SA 3.0*

September, Beatrix found the same rare fungus in a different place. She made two drawings, giving McIntosh one of them with a map drawn on the back showing where she'd discovered the fungi.

Even while she was away, Beatrix and her former governess, Annie Moore, kept up their correspondence. When she received word from Annie that little Noel was sick in bed, Beatrix decided to write him a picture letter on September 4, 1893, to cheer him up. She began with those now famous words, "My dear Noel, I don't know what to write to you, so I shall tell you a story about four little rabbits . . . ."

Beatrix had brought her new Belgian hare, Peter Piper, with her to Eastwood and undoubtedly used him as her model for the naughty Peter Rabbit character in her letter to Noel. Peter Piper was "bought at a very tender age, in the Uxbridge Road Shepherds Bush, for the exorbitant sum of 4/6" and Beatrix loved him dearly, later reminiscing that he was "an affectionate companion and a quiet friend." He would be forever immortalized in Beatrix's book *The Tale of Peter Rabbit*, but that would come later.

The next day, Beatrix wrote another letter to Noel's younger brother, Eric, because she didn't want him to feel left out. This time, however, the illustrated story featured a frog named Jeremy Fisher who tried to catch a tasty minnow but ended up with a sticky prickleback. The seeds for another book were planted.

As biographer Linda Lear states, "In the space of two days [Beatrix] had found and painted a rare and important mycological specimen and created two fictional characters that one day would be world-famous. Both were products of her skill as a naturalist, her acute observation of people and places, her creative imagination, and her sure sense of audience."

Beatrix didn't travel alone often, but right before her 28th birthday she was invited to visit her younger cousin, Caroline Hutton, and her family in Gloucestershire. Helen almost spoiled the trip by not letting her daughter go, saying the journey would be too much for Beatrix. But in the end, Caroline took charge and pulled Beatrix onto the train before her mother could object.

Caroline was an independent thinker, and Beatrix liked her beautiful cousin's fiery spirit. Caroline did have some definite opinions, however, and Beatrix didn't always agree with her. Once when Caroline pronounced her "dislike of babies and all child cousins" within the family, Beatrix wrote, "Latter day fate ordains that many women shall be unmarried and self-contained, nor should I personally dream to complain, but I hold an old-fashioned notion that a happy marriage is the crown of a woman's life."

The Moore Children

Edwin and Annie Carter Moore had eight children: Noel, Eric, Marjorie, Winifred (Freda), Norah (Bardy), Joan, Hilda, and Beatrix. Annie's husband was gone often with his job as a civil engineer, sometimes for as long as six months at a time, so Annie had the main role in raising the family. She was very strict and brought up the children with strong religious values and teachings. Both the boys and girls were sent to schools for their education, and they all enjoyed music, family games, parties, and visits from special friends like Beatrix Potter. Moreover, two of the girls, Norah and Joan, visited Beatrix at Hill Top in 1912.

Noel contracted polio when he was nine, and he always had a limp. After finishing his schooling, he became an Anglo-Catholic priest and worked with children from poor families in the East End of London. He never married but spent his life serving others.

Eric Moore got a civil engineering degree, but his career was put on hold while he served in the Royal Engineers during World War I. He was gassed in the war and was awarded the Military

(continued on next page)

(continued from previous page)

Cross and Bar. After the war, he returned to his civil engineering work, married, and had three children. After retirement, he became a farmer.

Marjorie Moore became a naval nurse and served on board a battleship, and Freda taught piano lessons and, when she was in her 40s, married a widowed engineer. Norah went to the London Royal Academy of Music and played cello; later she taught crafting classes at an isolated South African mission. Joan Moore worked in London hospitals helping the poor, while Hilda married a doctor and had three children. She died at an early age from multiple sclerosis.

Beatrix, the baby of the family and Beatrix Potter's goddaughter, also earned a certificate from the London Royal Academy of Music, taught music in South Africa, became a journalist after she returned to England, and later married another journalist from Sweden. She lived until 1996. Beatrix Potter had hoped to send one or two of the Moore girls to college one day, but it never worked out.

Beatrix was rather surprised at her cousin's views on matrimony and children, as Caroline's parents obviously had a loving marriage and the Hutton home was warm and caring. In any case, the visit was one Beatrix would always remember, and the two young women maintained a lifelong friendship.

Beatrix continued to study and paint fungi over the next two years, eventually creating more than 300 illustrations. She also focused on geology and paleontology and spent a good bit of time at London's Natural History Museum. Beatrix was indeed a talented illustrator, but she was also becoming an expert in several fields of scientific study.

As a young man, Bertram obviously had more freedom than his sister and usually came and went as he pleased. He had completed his college studies at Oxford in the summer of 1893, and afterward chose to become a landscape painter. He still shared many of his sister's interests, and the two enjoyed fossil hunting on their family trip to Falmouth on England's Cornish coast in the spring of 1894, and again during their summer vacation at Lennel, Scotland. It was the last year that Rupert would rent a house in Scotland, yet Bertram, who was drawn to the Scottish countryside, would later move there permanently.

As for Beatrix, she continued her self-study and paintings of fungi, lichens, fossils, and archeological artifacts, and with each year the detail in her drawings became more refined and realistic. In late 1895, Caroline

Martineau, a family acquaintance and principal of Morley Memorial College, commissioned Beatrix to create 12 lithographs, or color prints, of insects to be used in a presentation. Beatrix gained a great deal of knowledge about the printing and publishing process during her work as a scientific illustrator, and she was encouraged by the good reviews.

Soon after, Beatrix painted and offered some frog illustrations, based on the Jeremy Fisher picture letter she'd written to Eric Moore in 1893, to a German firm of art printers named Ernest Nister. The firm had bought some of her earlier drawings, and she thought it might be interested in publishing the frog illustrations in booklet form. The firm responded that it didn't think anyone would be interested in a booklet about frogs. Nonetheless, Ernest Nister did buy the illustrations to use in one of its children's magazines—but only after Beatrix negotiated a price to her liking, proving she was already becoming a savvy businesswoman. At almost 30 years of age, she was finally feeling more independent and stronger in mind and body.

In the summer of 1895, the Potters returned to the Lake District, and Beatrix continued her focus on mycology, the study of mushrooms and fungi. By this point, she had moved from just illustrating fungi and lichens (a combination of fungi and algae) to learning how they

Royal Botanic Gardens, Kew, between 1890 and 1900. *Library of Congress Prints and Photographs Division, LC-DIG-ppmsc-08589*

reproduced. Until this time, mycologists had given very little thought to how the spores on mushrooms or fungi germinate, or grow and spread. Beatrix believed that she could germinate some spores herself, but first she wanted to do more research.

When Beatrix returned to London, her uncle, Sir Henry Roscoe, helped her get a student ticket to the Royal Botanic Gardens at Kew so she could visit and study there. The facility, also known simply as Kew Gardens, was only open to scientists working on special projects. Her uncle also introduced her to the director of Kew Gardens, Mr. Thistleton-Dyer, and George Massee, a principal assistant, who "seemed to like her drawings."

Beatrix visited Kew often, learning more each time she went. She carried her new knowledge back to the Lake District the next summer, along with a new camera and a better microscope. She experimented, corresponded with Charlie McIntosh, observed, recorded results in her journal, painted specimens, and finally succeeded in germinating the spores of gill fungi.

Beatrix had a theory, one that had never been discussed before. She reasoned that fungi have an under-

"I think one of my pleasantest memories of Esthwaite is sitting on Oatmeal Crag on a Sunday afternoon, where there is sort of a table rock with a dip, with the lane and fields and oak copse like in a trough below my feet, and all the little tiny fungus people singing and bobbing and dancing in the grass and under the leaves all down below, like the whistling that some people cannot hear of stray mice and bats, and I sitting up above and knowing something about them."

—*Beatrix Potter's journal, September 21, 1896*

ground form, a mold, and this enables them to spread. Back in London, she explained her results and theory to Uncle Henry and then wondered if anyone at Kew had ever had the same results. None of them had. Furthermore, most of the gentleman who worked there disregarded and dismissed Beatrix's work.

Both she and Uncle Henry were disappointed. Neither of them wanted someone else to later claim her work, so with her uncle's encouragement, Beatrix wrote a paper detailing her theory and research called, "On the Germination of the Spores of *Agaricineae*, by Miss Helen B. Potter." During the writing process, Beatrix continued round-the-clock research, observation, and record keeping to ensure her results were accurate. When both she and Uncle Henry were satisfied that her paper was complete, they wanted to submit it to the Linnean Society of London, the world's oldest active biological society, for possible publication.

George Massee, who had begun to agree with Beatrix's results when he, too, was able to sprout several of her spores, agreed to submit the paper to the general secretary of the society on March 18, 1897, on her behalf. As a woman, Beatrix couldn't be a member of the society nor attend the April 1, 1897, meeting when her paper was to be read. Once again, her theories were not taken very seriously. In a letter to Charlie McIntosh, however, she stated, "My paper was read at the Linnean Society . . . but they say it requires more work in it before it is printed."

It's unclear exactly what happened, but the paper was never published. Records show that Beatrix withdrew the paper a week after its presentation, and the original has never been found. Despite the disappointing outcome, Beatrix did what no other amateur or female mycologist of the time had done—she had a scientific paper read in front of the all-male Linnean Society. Ironically, her theories about the reproduction of fungi are now widely accepted, and the society issued a posthumous apology to Beatrix in 1997 for the unfair treatment she was given a century earlier. Her realistic fungi illustrations are still used in textbooks today.

Beatrix's journal ended about the time she was getting ready to submit her paper to the Linnean Society, so any record of her feelings afterward is lost. It also seems that the door to her intense focus on the study of fungi closed after her theory on fungi reproduction and spores was rejected. Beatrix always remained interested and knowledgeable about many scientific fields—mycology, archeology, paleontology, geology, botany, and entomology—but her creative career was about to take another turn, one that would make her world-famous.

In addition to writing charming picture letters to the Moore children and some of her own young cousins, Beatrix had continued sketching whimsical animal scenes to amuse herself and painting pictures of rabbit families for nurseries. She'd also continued to look for opportunities do some commercial art and to "market her fanciful drawings of pets for greeting cards or booklets. She wanted to make her own money instead of being dependent on her parents, especially as her father Rupert's health was declining and he was becoming more difficult.

During a visit to the Moore home in early 1900, Annie suggested that Beatrix should try to create children's books based on the picture letters she'd sent to the children through the years. They'd kept them all and would be happy to lend them back to Beatrix. This was an appealing idea, and Beatrix agreed. Her brother Bertram also encouraged her to start the project, so she began with the Peter Rabbit picture letter she'd sent to Noel in 1893.

Beatrix made pen-and-ink drawings in black and white of the original illustrations on other sheets of paper, then rewrote and expanded the text into the charming, yet suspenseful, story of a disobedient little rabbit, dressed in "real people clothes," who has a scary adventure in Mr. McGregor's garden. She added more black-and-white illustrations, copied everything into a stiff exercise book, and painted one colored illustration on the front. She now had what she considered to be a proper book to submit to publishers.

Next, Beatrix consulted her old friend, Hardwicke Rawnsley, because he'd published several children's books and knew about the process. He thought her book

Beatrix created examples or dummy copies of her books to show publishers how they would look. *Beatrix Potter dummy manuscripts by Jack1956 is marked with CC0 1.0*

was excellent. Upon his advice and encouragement, Beatrix sent her little manuscript, titled *The Tale of Peter Rabbit and Mr. McGregor's Garden* to six publishers, including Frederick Warne & Co., which had shown interest in her work years earlier.

Before long, she had six rejections. Some of the publishers had no interest, some specified a different length or larger book size, and others said they wouldn't consider her manuscript without fully colored illustrations.

But Beatrix had her own ideas of how her book should look. She'd loved Anna Barbauld's tiny, child-sized books when she was young and was inspired to create something similar that would fit easily into small hands. She also knew that using only colored illustrations would drive the printing costs of the book too high.

Beatrix wrote a letter to Marjorie Moore on March 13, 1900, and said: "[Miss Potter] would rather make 2 or 3 little books costing 1/- each, than one big book costing 6/- because she thinks little rabbits cannot afford to spend 6 shillings on one book, and would never buy it." Beatrix was determined to have the book just as she wanted, so she decided to have it printed privately. In 1901, she visited a London printer, Strangeways & Sons, and arranged for it to print 250 copies of the book she was now simply calling *The Tale of Peter Rabbit*. She also ordered 42 zinc blocks made by another company for the black-and-white illustrations inside the book and commissioned a firm called Hentschel to create a three-colored set of blocks needed to print the illustration on the front cover. At last, Strangeways & Sons had everything it needed to move forward.

In the meantime, Hardwicke Rawnsley continued trying to get Beatrix's rabbit book into the hands of a traditional publisher. With Beatrix's permission, he rewrote her story into rhyming verse. It was a charming version, and he sent it to Frederick Warne & Co. in September 1901, hoping the firm would reconsider the alternate adaptation. Apparently, it seriously considered the project but still wanted fewer, full-color illustrations. Moreover, the firm decided it was too late in the year to do anything, so all discussions were put off for the time being.

On December 16, 1901, the first privately printed copies of *The Tale of Peter Rabbit* were done. Beatrix gave her books as gifts to family and friends, and the story was an immediate success. Other people wanted copies as well, so she sold them for the "modest sum of 1/2d." Before long, Beatrix ran out of books and needed to arrange for a second printing of 200 copies. She made just a few minor changes to the text, and the books were delivered in February 1902.

While Beatrix was in the middle of having her little book privately printed, Frederick Warne & Co. decided to move forward with negotiations after all. The firm stated that it preferred Beatrix's original text over Rawnsley's verse, but if Miss Potter was willing to redraw the illustrations in color and cut the number of pictures in the book, it would publish it.

After much consideration and negotiations to keep the book small and affordable, Beatrix agreed to the publisher's request. She was paired with the youngest Warne son in the firm, Norman, to work on what he called Beatrix's "bunny book," and she signed the contract in June 1902. Eight thousand copies of the Warne edition of *The Tale of Peter Rabbit* were printed, and they were released on October 2, 1902, when Beatrix was 36 years old.

The book was a winner from the start. It was sold in all the London bookshops and featured in the Warne book catalog, where it received "top billing in the list of new books." It had to be reprinted several times, and by the end of 1903, more than 50,000 copies of Beatrix's book had been sold!

Beatrix always claimed that *The Tale of Peter Rabbit* was a success because the story had been "written to a child—not made to order." Yet, whatever her secret ingredient of storytelling and illustrating was, Beatrix was now on the road to recognition.

MORE LITTLE BOOKS, LOVE, AND LOSS

---

*"I thought my story had come right with patience &
waiting."* —BEATRIX POTTER, *in a letter to Millie
Warne, February 1, 1906*

Beatrix's collaboration with Norman Warne on *The
Tale of Peter Rabbit* was just the first of many. His
brothers, Harold and Fruing, were also part of the firm,
but they were both married with families and had more
responsibilities. Therefore, they left the "bunny book"
project to Norman, more or less to give him something
to do.

The company's founder and Norman's father, Frederick Warne, passed away in November 1901. Norman,

who was 33, unmarried, and living with his widowed mother and older sister Millie at the family home at No. 8 Bedford Square when he first met Beatrix, was the youngest Warne child and undoubtedly his mother's "baby." He was also a favorite with all of his nieces and nephews, and by all accounts a good-natured, handsome young man.

Of course, the relationship between editor and author was quite formal at the beginning. Beatrix and Norman exchanged countless letters during contract negotiations and the publication process, many with the prim greeting, "Dear Sir." And when they met in person, they always had a chaperone, as was proper by Victorian standards. From the outset, however, Beatrix knew her own mind and wasn't afraid to voice her opinions. She wanted to be involved in every step of the book's decision-making and production, even when she was traveling.

Beatrix also had more ideas for books, and by Christmas of 1901, she had written a new story based on a tale about a poor tailor in the town of Gloucestershire whose work was mysteriously completed for him by mice when he fell ill. It was a tale she'd almost certainly heard of during one of her visits to see her cousin Caroline, and it intrigued her immediately. While working on the story, she even visited a tailor's shop in the Chelsea area of London to have a button repaired. In truth, she'd pulled the button off herself to create the excuse, because she wanted to observe the inside of the tailor's shop and watch the tailor work. She noticed "his tools and the snippets and odds and ends which surrounded him, and later made sketches of what she had seen."

However, Beatrix figured it was too soon to pitch another book proposal to Warne, as *Peter Rabbit* wouldn't be released until the following October. So, Beatrix copied the story into another stiff-covered exercise book, created 12 watercolor illustrations to go with the text, and presented it to Freda Moore as a Christmas gift. Sometime in 1902, Beatrix borrowed the picture book back with the intention of printing *The Tailor of Gloucester* privately, as she'd done with her first book. In her mind, the "tale was a fairy story with a 'happy ever after' ending," and she always claimed this "mouse book" was her favorite.

Therefore, she redrew some of the pictures, edited the text, commissioned 16 colored blocks for the illustrations from Hentschel, and took it to Strangeways & Sons to be printed. She ordered 500 copies and asked that it be formatted like *The Tale of Peter Rabbit*. The title page for this self-published version of *The Tailor of Gloucester* was marked December 1902.

So, in early 1902, the production of the *Peter Rabbit* book was underway, and Beatrix was already working out the particulars for getting her "mouse book" privately printed. She'd already informed Norman that she was committed to self-publishing the first edition of *The Tailor of Gloucester,* especially since she thought he'd want to cut out most of her rhymes and the tailor! By mutual agreement, they discussed ideas for other little books instead.

Norman liked one idea in particular, a tale about the adventures of a rascally rodent named Squirrel Nutkin and the colony of red squirrels around Derwentwater, a large lake in England's Lake District. The story, based on letters to Noel Moore in 1897 and his sister Norah in 1901, was a charming one featuring squirrels on little rafts who used their tails as sails to move across the lake to Owl Island, taking presents to Old Brown, the owl.

With Norman's encouragement, Beatrix borrowed back the more complete picture letter she'd sent to Norah and began revising and expanding the story and illustrations. With two books in the works, Beatrix was a busy young woman, but it seemed she thrived on the fast pace she was keeping while creating two books at the same time. She also realized she needed a model to use to paint her squirrel pictures, so she headed to a pet store.

She wrote to Norman, "I bought two [squirrels] but they weren't a pair, and fought so frightfully that I had to get rid of the handsomer—and most savage one—The other squirrel is rather a nice little animal, but half of one ear has been bitten off, which spoils his appearance!"

She also seemed to be having trouble drawing Old Mr. Brown, the owl, even after visiting the London Zoological Gardens and sketching the owls there. But, in another letter to Norman, she reassured him that, "I am going to meet my brother at the Lakes tomorrow; I think *he* could very likely improve that owl."

Beatrix was certainly glad to see Bertram on her trip to the Lake District, but she had to be worried about him as well. In addition to developing a drinking problem in his late teens or early 20s, he'd also been living a secret life in Scotland, without his parents' knowledge. He'd fallen in love with a wine merchant's daughter named Mary Welsh Scott and eloped with her to Edinburgh, where they married on November 20, 1902. He had also become a farmer, in addition to painting landscapes. Bertram and Mary lived in Ancrum, a village in the Scottish Borders area, and it seems they had a happy marriage.

It's unclear if Beatrix initially knew about her brother's marriage, but even if she had, she never would have disclosed the information to their parents. Although she may have still been under their strict supervision at the age of 36, Bertram had escaped the often oppressive environment at 2 Bolton Gardens. He sometimes joined the family on vacations, obviously coming without Mary after his marriage, but Rupert and Helen would not find out about his wife until he'd been married for almost 11 years.

Beatrix was a frequent guest at the Warne offices on Bedford Street at Covent Garden, and she and Norman were becoming good friends. Their letters also started having a less formal tone, and Beatrix was quite agreeable when Norman suggested they traditionally publish a shorter version of her privately printed book, *The Tailor of Gloucester*. Beatrix even found time to visit the South Kensington Museum (today the Victoria and Albert Museum) and sketch the "most beautiful 18th century clothing" in preparation for new illustrations.

Despite the slowly changing relationship between editor and author, Beatrix still maintained a watchful eye over every part of her two books' production. She was

Frontispiece of the Tailor Mouse for Beatrix's 1902 book, *The Tailor of Gloucester*. Photo © Tate

even concerned about the detail of selecting endpapers and bindings. It was decided that, just as *The Tale of Peter Rabbit* had been issued in both paper binding and cloth binding for a deluxe edition, *The Tailor of Gloucester* and *The Tale of Squirrel Nutkin* would be done the same way. Beatrix was proud that the calico cloth for the deluxe editions would be obtained from Edmund Potter & Co., the company Grandfather Potter had started.

As biographer Linda Lear noted, "For the first time [Beatrix] got up in the morning with something purposeful to do. She had publishers to visit, proofs to approve, places she needed to visit to sketch, small but meaningful affairs to manage."

Finally, all the edits, revisions, and illustrations were completed, and publication dates for the books were set. *Squirrel Nutkin* would be published in August 1903, and the Warne version of *The Tailor of Gloucester* would be published in October. Beatrix was satisfied with the work she had done, her confidence grew, and she had money of her own. She had many ideas and hoped Frederick Warne & Co. would continue publishing more of her little books.

By July 1903, Beatrix's two books were out of her hands and in the production phase. She wrote to Norman, "I had been a little hoping too that something might be said about another book."

A reply came back to Beatrix, but it was from Norman's brother Harold. Norman was away on business, but Harold said he would be happy to discuss a new book idea with her.

That was not what Beatrix wanted to hear! It was Norman whom she wanted to talk to—not his brother. After two attempts to get Beatrix to discuss her idea with him, Harold finally managed to persuade her to share her thoughts by a letter sent from the Lake District where she was staying. She envisioned another rabbit story—a sequel of sorts to *The Tale of Peter Rabbit*.

Beatrix was already a very important author for the firm, so her ideas were carefully considered. Moreover, any suggestions or requests she made to correct mistakes in book proofs were taken care of immediately. Harold did what he could to keep Beatrix happy, but when Norman returned to London, she was glad to be back in touch with her favorite editor. He told her that *Squirrel Nutkin* was a success and that he liked her idea for another rabbit story. They would start collaborating immediately.

In the meantime, Beatrix also began what she would call her "side shows" for merchandise associated with the characters from her books. She designed and sewed a Peter Rabbit doll and registered the patent on December 28, 1903. Later, she created wallpaper, china figurines, board games, and eventually, other fun things like painting books. She was wise to think of patents, as the Peter Rabbit and Friends merchandise would make a lot

A few editions of Beatrix's little books. *Attribution-NoDerivs 2.0 Generic (CC BY-ND 2.0)*

of money over the years. These side shows would prove to be just as important as the little books themselves.

Unfortunately for Beatrix, Warne failed to secure a copyright on *The Tale of Peter Rabbit* book in America, and pirated editions and sequels began to be published. This oversight cost Beatrix—and Warne & Co.—a lot of money, so it's no wonder that she became extremely careful with anything associated with her creations.

On the whole, however, Beatrix's royalty checks from the sales of her books were increasing, and she was quickly becoming wealthy. She arranged to be paid once a month, and it's probable that she was already considering buying property in the Lake District at this point. It had taken a long time, but Beatrix was now an independent woman who could afford to make her own decisions, without her parents' input or consent.

The Tale of Benjamin Bunny was published in 1904 and featured Peter and his cousin Benjamin as they went back to Mr. McGregor's garden to retrieve the clothes Peter left behind in the first book. Again, Beatrix used suspense and humor to create another successful story. It was followed the same year with *The Tale of Two Bad Mice*, a book about Hunca Munca and Tom Thumb, married mice who raided a dollhouse when the dolls were away. They became enraged when they discovered that the food on the dolls' table wasn't real and vandalized the dollhouse.

Beatrix's inspiration for Hunca Munca and Tom Thumb were two mice she had caught in her aunt and uncle's kitchen at their home in Gloucestershire and brought home earlier in the year. But she had also heard about the dollhouse that Norman had built for his niece Winifred Warne, Fruing's daughter, and the idea for the story had gelled in Beatrix's creative mind.

When she told Norman about her vision, he invited her to Fruing's house in Surbiton in February 1904 to see the dollhouse for herself and make sketches.

In the past, she'd visited the Warnes' home in Bedford Square, and she and Norman's sister Millie were becoming close friends. Beatrix already thought highly of Norman's mother and the rest of the Warne family too. She and Norman were also becoming close and slowly falling in love. Beatrix wanted to spend more time with him and his warm, loving family. They were everything Beatrix had ever admired in other families. But now she faced a dilemma: her mother, Helen, was having none of it.

Perhaps Helen sensed that her daughter was becoming a bit too attached to that "tradesman publisher" whom she worked with on her little books and his family. It just wouldn't do, as the Warnes were certainly not on the same social level as the Potters. Beatrix could not believe her mother's hypocrisy. Hadn't both the Potters and Leeches once been tradesmen? Moreover, the Warnes were a fine, upstanding, and well-respected London family.

It didn't make sense, but once again, Beatrix tried to be the dutiful daughter. She declined Norman's invitation to go to Surbiton but worried that the Warnes might think her "uncivil" and rude. In the end, Norman provided photographs of the dollhouse for Beatrix to reference, and she dedicated the book to Winifred when it was finished.

By March 1904, Beatrix and Norman were writing letters to each other every day, and of course, they discussed ideas for Beatrix's upcoming books to be published in 1905. One was *The Tale of Mrs. Tiggy-Winkle*, a story about a hedgehog and based on Kitty MacDonald, the Dalguise washerwoman Beatrix remembered from her childhood. The other was *The Tale of the Pie and the Patty-Pan*, which was set in the village of Sawrey, featured Ribby the cat, and focused on the complicated tea party she held for Duchess the dog.

Norman and Beatrix worked diligently on the newest little books, and she concentrated on drawing, and often redrawing, the illustrations and tweaking story text until Norman finally expressed his approval in June 1905. Beatrix noted that *The Tale of the Pie and Patty-Pan* was her second favorite book, after *The Tailor of Gloucester*.

With the hard work of completing the books behind her, Beatrix would soon be traveling to Wales with her family for their 1905 summer vacation. However, she did write to Norman to say that she would "like to get some new work fixed before going away to Wales." She wanted to know what she would be doing next so she could start on it.

Beatrix received Norman's reply before she left London, and his letter contained a big surprise. He asked her to marry him! Beatrix was elated and accepted his proposal right away. At some point, Norman presented her with an engagement ring before the Potters left for Wales. But even though she was 39 years old, Beatrix figured she was in for a huge battle for her happiness with her parents.

She was right. Rupert and Helen were furious! They refused to give their consent, and although it seems ridiculous that a woman nearing 40 would need her parents' permission to get married, it was the common practice of the time. For one, the Potters did not approve of Norman as a match for their daughter, as he was a "lowly tradesman." But they also didn't want to lose the one person who could take care of them in their old age.

Beatrix wasn't a rebellious daughter, but she refused to break her engagement with Norman. In the end, Rupert and Helen asked her not to make a formal announcement until they returned from Wales, no doubt hoping their daughter would change her mind. Beatrix agreed to their request to keep the proposal a secret, although she would continue to wear Norman's engagement ring. She could hardly wait to become Mrs. Norman Warne and leave 2 Bolton Gardens forever. Happiness was only a few months away.

It wasn't to be. Shortly after the Potters left for Wales, Norman became deathly sick. Beatrix received a telegram from the Warnes on the morning of August 25, 1905, informing her of Norman's sudden illness and asking her to come back to London. But it was too late. Norman died that same afternoon in his bedroom in the Warne family's Bedford Square home from pernicious anemia or leukemia. He had just turned 37, and it had only been one month since he'd asked Beatrix to be his wife.

Beatrix was devastated. Her dream slowly turned into a nightmare as she silently mourned the only man she'd ever loved. She'd waited and been patient, hoping "for her story to come out right." It was not the ending she would have written.

From London to the
Lake District

"I must try to make a fresh beginning next year."
—BEATRIX POTTER, *in a letter to Millie Warne,*
December 23, 1905

Norman's death was the beginning of a new phase in Beatrix's life. She couldn't grieve for him openly, as very few people even knew they'd been engaged—and her parents wouldn't have stood for it in their home anyway. But at least she still had Norman's sister, Millie, as a confidante, and they wrote each other often.

In September, Millie invited Beatrix to stay with her and her mother for a few days. It was comforting to Beatrix to be in Norman's home in Bedford Square, at least for a little while. For the rest of her life, she would continue to wear the ring he'd given her as a reminder of the happy times they shared.

Beatrix needed time to adjust to the terrible shock of losing her fiancé, so in October she returned to a place that was near to her heart: the Lake District. Even before Norman died, Beatrix had heard that a small working farm called Hill Top was for sale in the village of Near Sawrey, and it had been her dream since she was a teen to buy her own property in the beautiful north England countryside. She probably felt the tug of her family's roots as well, as her great-grandfather Abraham

Vintage postcard of Hill Top Farm in Near Sawrey, England. *Image used by permission of author*

Crompton had once owned a large tract of land near the small village.

With a small inheritance from her aunt and the money earned from the sales of her books, Beatrix didn't need help from her parents. In fact, she had already started negotiations to purchase the Lakeland property earlier in the summer and now, in November, it was hers. It's unclear how Rupert felt about his daughter's investment, but by this point Beatrix was determined to have her way. She had no plans to desert her parents or forget her obligation to help take care of them. She would live in London most of the time and visit Near Sawrey when she could. But right now, she needed to be at Hill Top Farm.

On October 10, 1905, Beatrix wrote to Harold Warne, "My purchase seems to be regarded as a huge joke; I have been going over my hill with a tape measure."

The joke was indeed on Beatrix. She didn't know it when she bought Hill Top Farm, but she had paid twice the amount for her property that the previous owner, a local speculator, had paid six months earlier. It was a mistake she would not make again!

Hill Top Farm was everything Beatrix wanted. It was a working farm of 34 acres, with a farmhouse, outbuildings, and an orchard. The farmhouse also came with the tenant farmer, John Cannon and his family. Beatrix knew she needed help to keep the farm running, so she asked Cannon to stay on as her farm manager, and he agreed.

Beatrix took temporary lodgings at Belle Green, a cottage not far from Hill Top, while she made plans to enlarge her farmhouse. She personally designed a new section to be built onto the small house for John Cannon and his family, while reserving the original farmhouse quarters for herself. In this part, she added a large library room, where several of her brother's paintings were set as panels in the walls.

She also built a small dairy on the property, created a larger garden in front of the house, and hired a quarry-man to lay out new walks and a Brathay flagstone path, which matched the four slabs of local slate that made up the front porch entrance. When all the changes were completed in 1906, Beatrix had a plaque made and placed on the front of the addition with her initials and the date. Norman's death still hurt, but at least now Beatrix had a new love, Hill Top Farm—and a new focus, farming.

Beatrix didn't want to be known as a city-born "offcomer," so she learned everything she could about farming and village life. She even had John Cannon buy some Herdwick sheep, "sixteen ewes so there [would] be lambs the next spring." She probably chose this particular breed on the advice of her old friend, Hardwicke Rawnsley.

Herdwicks were a strong breed, native to the Lake District, and they thrived in the harsher landscapes of the high fells, or mountains, in the area. Herdwicks

Herdwick sheep. *Mark Fosh from Watford, UK / CC BY (https://creative-commons.org/licenses/by/2.0)*

were also prized for their wool, but due to a drop in wool prices, many farmers had turned to other breeds of sheep in previous years. Some of them had given up fell farming completely and abandoned their land. Thus, the hardy Herdwicks were no longer there to graze and keep the overgrowth in check.

Conservationists like Rawnsley were concerned that without the sheep, the abandoned fell land would deteriorate and change the landscape forever. Therefore, he had worked hard to reestablish the old breed of Herd-wick sheep in the Lakeland area. He'd even founded the Herdwick Sheep Breeders Association in 1899. Beatrix shared Rawnsley's concerns and was trying to do her part to help. Within two years, she had more than 30 Herdwicks at Hill Top.

Beatrix still enjoyed animals. Along with her sheep, she kept sheepdogs to herd them and cows, pigs, ducks, and hens. In addition to her outside dogs, Beatrix always had at least one dog that was her special pet, usually a collie. Her first, and favorite, was a working collie named Kep, who was featured in her book *The Tale of Jemima Puddle-Duck*. Kep would be the first in a long line of collies, and Beatrix always considered this intelligent breed of dog a necessary addition to her farm.

Satisfied with her progress at Hill Top Farm, Beatrix went back to London and 2 Bolton Gardens, resigned to fulfill her role as her parents' caretaker. She returned to Near Sawrey when she could be spared for a few days, and each time she worked in her garden or walked up the slate path to the front door Hill Top, she felt as though she had come home.

After Norman's death, his brother Harold had finally convinced Beatrix to at least discuss ideas for some new little books. *The Tale of Mrs. Tiggy-Winkle* and *The Tale of the Pie and the Patty-Pan* were being released in October,

Beatrix's Gardening Life

Beatrix always loved nature and admired beautiful gardens, but she was a "late bloomer" of sorts when it came to creating her own garden at Hill Top Farm. To help with her grief after losing Norman, she spent time planning how she wanted the garden to look—drawing sketches; hiring men to help; adding pathways and a trellis; planting fruit trees, roses, flowers, shrubs, and vegetables; and reshaping the existing beds into the sizes she desired. It was always a work in progress, but Beatrix enjoyed the simple pleasures of gardening.

According to gardening expert and writer Marta McDowell, Beatrix "was not impressed with gardener's Latin," preferring instead to use the common, and more local sounding, names of plants. Other village gardeners were always willing to share advice and plants, and Beatrix appreciated both . . . although she wasn't above pilfering a few discarded plants from her neighbors' compost heaps or burn piles after they thinned them out of their gardens.

"I stole some 'honesty' yesterday," she wrote to Millie, "it was put to be burnt in a heap of

(continued on next page)

(continued from previous page)

garden refuse!" According to McDowell, honesty, or *Lunaria annua*, is a small, easy-to-grow plant with pink flowers. Beatrix must've found the irony of "stealing honesty" quite amusing.

Over time, Beatrix added many other varieties of plants and flowers including snowdrops, primrose, hyacinth, forsythia, flowering currant, Japanese quince, cowslip, wisteria, wild garlic, violets, periwinkle, lilac, columbine, snapdragons, ferns, iris, clematis, cranesbill, foxglove, hydrangea, lilies, roses, valerian, and more.

Beatrix's garden has now been restored to showcase how it probably looked during her lifetime, and visitors come from around the world to see it. It has been written up in countless gardening books and magazines and filmed, photographed, and documented in all seasons. Beatrix's beautiful Hill Top garden, with its unique green gate, lovely slate walls and paths, wooden trellises, beehive box, and many plants, flowers, and vegetables, still brings joy to anyone with a gardener's heart.

and it was time to start thinking about a new project. Of course, Beatrix was dreading working on a little book without Norman.

In a letter dated September 5, 1905, Beatrix wrote to Harold, "It will be a trying thing to come for the first time to the office, but there is no help for it." Beatrix was determined to move forward, however, and she went. They discussed *The Tale of Mr. Jeremy Fisher*, which was based on the "frog" picture letter Beatrix had written to Eric Moore from Eastwood on September 5, 1893, the day after she wrote the Peter Rabbit letter to his older brother Noel. As she told Harold, "I know some people don't like frogs! [sic] but I think I had convinced Norman that I could make it a really pretty book with a good many flowers & water plants for backgrounds. That book would be easy & plain sailing."

Harold agreed. Beatrix spent the first half of 1906 reworking the original picture letter text and painting colorful frog illustrations, all while supervising the remodeling work at Hill Top. It was a busy time for the author, but the book was released in July, right on schedule. *Jeremy Fisher*, however, wasn't her only ongoing project.

Beatrix was also creating two new books for her very youngest readers to be released in time for the 1906 Christmas season. *The Tale of Miss Moppet*, a kitten and mouse story about teasing, and *The Story of a Fierce Bad Rabbit*, a tale about the consequences of a naughty little rabbit's bad behavior, were first formatted in a panorama design. This meant the illustrations and text were printed on one long strip of paper that folded up into a small rectangle tied with ribbon. The stories were popular, but the panorama design was not, as shopkeepers constantly needed to refold the pages of the accordion-style book. Ultimately, Warne republished the newest little tales in the traditional book form.

Over the next eight years, Beatrix juggled her time between London and Near Sawrey. It wasn't always easy, as her aging parents depended more and more on her help and didn't want her to leave. She often felt torn between her role as a dutiful, 40-year-old spinster daughter and that of an author/illustrator/farmer, but Beatrix was trying to make the most of her life as it had turned out.

Nonetheless, these first years as the owner of Hill Top were Beatrix's golden years for writing. She published her little books at a steady pace: *The Tale of Tom Kitten* (1907), *The Tale of Jemima Puddle-Duck* (1908), *The Roly-Poly Pudding* (1908), *The Tale of the Flopsy Bunnies* (1909), *Ginger and Pickles* (1909), *The Tale of Mrs. Tittlemouse* (1910), *The Tale of Timmy Tiptoes* (1911), *The Tale of Mr. Tod* (1912), and *The Tale of Pigling Bland* (1913).

Several of the books were set at Hill Top Farm, either inside the house or out in the garden. Others featured Near Sawrey, and Beatrix often used her surroundings and the village scenes and buildings in her illustrations. The local residents grew accustomed to her walking through the village, sketchbook in hand, poking her head inside homes and stores, drawing whatever caught her fancy. It was often a point of pride to have one's kitchen, garden gate, or some personal item immortalized in one of Miss Potter's books.

Beatrix worked hard to become a skilled farmer. She continued to be interested in raising Herdwick sheep and learned everything she could about farm practices, animal science, and caring for the land. She followed John Cannon around when she was staying at Hill Top, asking questions and being very hands-on with the farm chores. But she had also become a shrewd businesswoman, interested in expanding her farm and land ownership.

She'd gained some hard-won experience when she purchased Hill Top Farm at an inflated price and realized it might be a good idea to consult with an expert before she bought any more land. Moreover, she wanted someone who was used to the sometimes-complicated transfer of Lake District property.

Therefore, in 1908, Beatrix visited the local, well-regarded firm of solicitors (or lawyers) W.H. Heelis & Son for advice. The firm had offices in both Hawkshead and Ambleside, and it was in Hawkshead that Beatrix met William Heelis, a slim, tall, quiet man, and a country rector's son. He was 38, quite handsome, and very easygoing.

Beatrix felt comfortable with William from the start, and when Castle Farm (with its farmhouse, Castle Cottage) became available for purchase the next year, she asked William to act as her solicitor. She could trust

Intrigue, Language, and Lingo

It's true that Frederick Warne & Co. targeted Beatrix's books at younger readers. However, it's also a fact that the vocabulary, story lines, and bits of intrigue she wove into her tales satisfied readers of all ages. They still do.

For example, the plots of her little stories may seem quite simple or even silly at times, but Beatrix addressed many serious themes and ideas in her books, including life and death, bad behavior and its consequences, disappointment, kindness, friendship, betrayal, industry, laziness, economics, tragedy, class, gender, vengeance, and more.

Beatrix also included some amazing vocabulary in her work. *Periwigs, pompadours, impertinence, muffatees, bolster, disconsolately, improvident, mournfully, conspicuous, perplexed, stile, punctually,* and *genteel* are among the words she masterfully inserted into the tales. According to biographer Leslie Linder, "Beatrix Potter loved unusual words and realized that children appreciated them also, although sometimes she used them against the advice of her publishers."

Perhaps the most famous of all her literary lingo

(continued on next page)

(continued from previous page)

is found in *The Tale of the Flopsy Bunnies* (1909): "It is said that the effect of eating too much lettuce is 'soporific'." Her illustration of sleeping bunnies provides the reader with a contextual clue. And of course, who doesn't associate drinking chamomile tea at bedtime with Peter and his mother?

Today, many people who are learning English as a second language find Beatrix's tales to be perfect for practice because the stories are easy to read yet full of first-rate plots, themes, and vocabulary that don't feel too young for more mature readers. No wonder fans from all over the world travel to the village of Near Sawrey and Hill Top Farm to visit the home of one of the most beloved authors of all time.

him to take care of all the business arrangements and contracts. On May 12, 1909, with William's assistance, Beatrix became the owner of Castle Farm, the property directly across from Hill Top.

William became Beatrix's legal advisor, and one who could act on her behalf concerning property matters when she was in London. And as Beatrix began to buy more land in the area, William was there to help her negotiate. They made a good team, and through their business interactions they slowly became friends. It was also during this period that Beatrix began to spend more of her time in Near Sawrey and less in London. She was happiest at Hill Top, and gradually her interest began to shift from being a creator of little books to becoming a Lakeland countrywoman, farmer, village resident, and landowner.

Beatrix and William spent a lot of time together and enjoyed each other's company. They had much in common, so it was only natural that their feelings toward each other became more affectionate. William was a gentleman; he was kind. He also respected Beatrix and admired her strong character and hardworking nature.

In many ways, William reminded Beatrix of Norman with his quiet, sweet personality. Both men also came from large, happy families, something Beatrix had always wanted. It wasn't long before the two fell in love, and William asked Beatrix to marry him in 1912. He was five years younger than Beatrix, 41 to her 46, but that didn't matter. She could hardly believe she'd been given a second chance at romance, and she accepted William's proposal.

Of course, she knew she was in for yet another battle for her happiness. Rupert and Helen would never approve of Beatrix's marriage to a mere tradesman, even though William was an esteemed solicitor from an old, respected Lakeland family. Beatrix chose to wait before telling her parents she was engaged, but when she did, they were outraged, just as she'd expected. She'd made up her mind, however, and decided to bide her time. Unsurprisingly, the stress from finishing up a book, working on the farm, and dealing with her parents' anger took its toll on Beatrix's health. She had always suffered from frequent illnesses, and her heart had been weak since her bout of rheumatic fever in her late teens, but in late 1912, Beatrix got very sick with pneumonia. Her parents insisted she return to 2 Bolton Gardens to recover, and Beatrix was too ill to argue. It would be a long time before she was well enough to return to Near Sawrey, so she looked forward to receiving William's letters. Rupert and Helen still wouldn't talk about Beatrix's marriage, once again hoping it would be called off.

When the elder Potters expressed their negative feelings about William's proposal, help and encouragement arrived in the form of an unexpected ally. Bertram came home and finally confessed to his parents that he'd been married for more than 10 years. He insisted that Beatrix should have the same opportunity to marry whomever she wanted. Rupert and Helen were shocked, but eventually they gave their reluctant permission for Beatrix to marry William.

Millie Warne also reassured Beatrix that her family was happy to hear the good news. Beatrix didn't want the Warnes to think she was being disloyal to Norman's memory, so Millie's message put those fears to rest. Of course, Norman would want Beatrix's happiness.

At last, Beatrix's health improved, and she returned to Hill Top Farm—and to William—in April 1913. She was back home and ready to make plans to become Mrs. Heelis.

Mrs. Heelis

"There is a great deal of work in the illustrations. It is much easier for me to attend to real live pigs & rabbits."
—Beatrix Potter, *in a letter to Miss Wyatt, November 15, 1920*

Hill Top had never been Beatrix's full-time residence. It was a peaceful getaway and a haven for her creativity, and she wanted to keep it that way. It would also be too small and cramped for a married couple, and she had no desire to change it. Therefore, she decided that she and William would live at Castle Cottage after they got married. She started the process of updating their new home-to-be, but she and William still had not set a wedding date.

Beatrix continued to travel back and forth from Near Sawrey to London to help care for her parents, and they

Beatrix in front of Hill Top farmhouse, 1913. *WorldPhotos / Alamy Stock Photo*

still struggled with the idea of accepting William as their son-in-law, balking at inviting him to their home. They also wanted Beatrix to put off the wedding indefinitely, but another personal illness in the fall "made her realize that she had to act or the cycle would endlessly repeat itself." She loved her parents, but it was time to move forward. Beatrix and William made plans to get married in mid-October 1913.

Apparently, the Potters warmed up to the young Lakeland lawyer as Beatrix wrote to a friend in September, "William has actually been invited up for a weekend soon—they never say much but they cannot dislike him."

William *was* likeable. Although he was very shy and quiet, he was pleasant and involved in village activities, enjoying sports, hunting, fishing, and country dancing. He often rode his motorcycle to visit Beatrix at Hill Top Farm and liked being outside, just as Beatrix did. He was considered a very eligible bachelor in the area, and many wondered why he had chosen a 46-year-old London-born eccentric spinster to be his wife. In truth, the two were well matched, and they looked forward to a happy marriage.

Ironically, Beatrix's *Pigling Bland* book was released just days before she got married, and many readers thought she had written her own "happily ever after" into the story. But Beatrix denied that the illustration of the two happy pigs arm-in-arm at the end was a portrait of her and William. She later wrote that if she wanted to put William in a book, "it [would] have to be some very tall thin animal."

Helen Beatrix Potter and William Heelis were married on Wednesday, October 15, 1913, at St. Mary Abbots, a parish church near the Potter home in Kensington, London. She was finally a bride at the age of 47. It was a small, quiet wedding, and apparently even their friends knew nothing about it. That probably suited Beatrix just fine. She was Mrs. Heelis now, and that was all that mattered. Rupert documented the occasion by taking photographs of the couple on the day before their wedding.

Beatrix and William were going to take a short honeymoon before returning to Near Sawrey. According to Annie Moore's youngest daughter Beatrix, named for her godmother Beatrix Potter, the couple stopped at the Moore home for a quick visit before they left London. The children were all amused to learn that the Heelis newlyweds planned to "collect a new white bull when they arrived at the railroad station at Windermere."

When Hill Top's farm manager John Cannon met them at the station with the bull, he addressed Beatrix as Miss Potter. She instantly corrected him, "I am Mrs. Heelis now." And indeed, from her wedding day onward, Beatrix insisted on being called by her married name. She had a different identity, and one that was far removed from that of the lonely, little girl she'd been at

A wedding photo of William and Beatrix Heelis, October 1913. © *Victoria and Albert Museum, London*

2 Bolton Gardens. According to biographer Linda Lear, "Beatrix began her new life as Mrs. Heelis with a quiet confidence in who she was and what she was about."

After a short honeymoon holiday, the couple temporarily stayed in a rented cottage in Near Sawrey until their home renovation was complete. Beatrix and William were finally able to move into Castle Cottage at the beginning of 1914, and they settled into daily life once more—but this time with each other.

Castle Cottage, where Beatrix and William lived after their marriage. *Image used by permission of author*

Rupert was very ill with stomach cancer, and Beatrix returned to London often in the early part of 1914 to see him. He passed away on May 8, 1914, with Helen and Beatrix by his side. Although Rupert had grown more difficult as he aged, Beatrix had been close to her father, especially when she was a child. She mourned her loss, but also worried what she would do now about her mother. In the end, they leased a house for Helen in Near Sawrey for a year, and Beatrix's aunt came to be her companion. It wasn't an ideal arrangement, as Beatrix still had to check on her demanding mother, but at least she didn't need to continually travel back to 2 Bolton Gardens to do so.

Prior to her father's death, Beatrix had been working on a book called *The Tale of Kitty-in-Boots*, but due to her hectic schedule she was unable to finish it in 1914. In fact, the book wouldn't be published until 2016. Therefore, for first time since 1902, Beatrix didn't have a little book ready for the Christmas season. She wrote to Harold Warne in May 1915, "My eyes are gone so long sighted & not clear nearby. . . . I suppose I shall have to take to spectacles, but I had better get properly fitted in London—a place I have no wish to go at present."

Beatrix had good reason to want to stay at home in the Lake District. The Great War—World War I—had begun the year before, and everything felt unsettled, even in remote villages like Near Sawrey. Like everyone else, she was saddened to hear of the deaths of so many of Britain's young servicemen. She was thankful when Bertram had been refused because of poor health when he tried to enlist in 1915. She was even more relieved when William, after receiving call-up papers, was excused because of his age and an old knee injury.

Beatrix even lost her beloved Kep, the faithful and loyal collie, that year—and she began to question her trust in Frederick Warne & Co. in regard to book sales and royalties. She had not received any royalty payments from her books for a long time, nor a royalty statement since 1911. She sensed something might be wrong, but Harold wrote to reassure her that all was well—it was just that money flow had been restricted due to the war.

Beatrix knew the issue had begun long before the war, so she wrote to Fruing next and received her money. She was still suspicious about Harold's inefficiency but decided to let the matter rest for the time being. Surprisingly, Beatrix never involved William in her writing and publishing concerns nor asked for his advice about this part of her life, because she knew he "had little patience for bad business practices." In turn, William seemed content to let his independent wife handle her own affairs.

In the meantime, the couple did their part for the war effort. William was busy with his business, but 50-year-old Beatrix and John Cannon, who also was getting up in age, tried to keep the farm going by planting crops and tending to animals. They soon realized they would need help with the farmwork, but almost all able-bodied young men were away fighting in the war. Beatrix began to think about hiring a woman to help, because she had 112 acres, large gardens, an orchard, and many heads of livestock to tend.

Beatrix was familiar with the Women's Land Army which had been created to promote the use of female labor during the war. One newspaper article "urged farmers not only to hire women to work on the land, but to offer them adequate wages." In March 1916, Beatrix hired a woman named Miss Eleanor Louisa Choyce, nicknamed Louie, to come to Hill Top to help with the farmwork. Louie was a governess around the age of 40 who was in between jobs. She proved to be an excellent worker and lifelong friend.

In a letter to her mother, Louie painted a picture of her employers and their life in the small English village: "[S]he is quite out of the common . . . short, blue-eyed, fresh-coloured face, frizzy hair brushed tightly back, dresses in a tweed skirt pinned at the back with a safety-pin. . . . Mr. Heelis is a quiet man, very kind. They believe in the simple life."

Louie lived at Hill Top instead of Castle Cottage, as Beatrix said William would feel more comfortable with the arrangement. Nevertheless, the two women worked busily through the spring and summer, with Louie leaving only after they'd gotten the planting done on time. She planned to return the following spring, and Beatrix was sad to see her new friend depart.

National Service Women's Land Army poster: GOD SPEED THE PLOUGH AND THE WOMAN WHO DRIVES IT. / H.G. Gawthorn; D.A. & S. Ld. London. *Library of Congress Prints and Photographs Division, USALC-USZC4-11192*

Beatrix was tired but satisfied with what she was accomplishing during the years of fighting. She was not, however, satisfied with Frederick Warne & Co. The fear she'd had about Harold's management of the company in 1915 was well founded, and by 1917, a scandal had erupted. Beatrix would step in to help to keep the publisher from going bankrupt.

Harold Warne, age 56, was arrested on charges of fraud in April 1917 as he was walking down the street near his office with his brother Fruing. He was "accused of passing £20,000 worth of forged bills and diverting money from the [Frederick Warne & Co.] publishing house into a failed fishing company he had inherited" from his mother. Now both companies were in deep financial trouble.

Harold pled guilty and was sentenced to 18 months of hard labor in prison. Beatrix felt betrayed, but she was also glad that she'd taken the legal steps earlier to keep the illustrations and copyrights of her books safe. Fruing, who wasn't involved in any way, was left to pick up the pieces of the crumbling publishing company. He had to sell the firm's property, as well as his own house and personal assets, to stop foreclosure. He and his family were devastated and stunned by what had happened.

Beatrix wanted to honor Norman's memory, and she also felt a loyalty to the company that had taken a chance on her when she was a young author and illustrator. She wanted to help Frederick Warne & Co. survive this tragedy. She rummaged through all her old illustrations and incomplete projects from past years to see what she could come up with and proposed a book of nursery rhymes. The pictures had been drawn at different times and the stories were pieced together, but she thought it would make a pretty book. She also created one new painting book and revised another for re-release. Fruing jumped at the chance to publish them.

Tom Kitten's Painting Book came out in June 1917, while *Appley Dapply's Nursery Rhymes* and a revised edition of *Peter Rabbit's Painting Book* were released in October. All three books sold very well. Beatrix helped Frederick Warne & Co. recover and rebuild, and she agreed that any money she was owed could be paid to her in company shares and long-term payments with interest. She did, however, insist on one condition: that Harold Warne "never meddles again."

Beatrix also published *The Tale of Johnny Town-Mouse* in 1918, and eventually the relationship between publisher and author was rebuilt and her trust in Frederick Warne & Co. was restored.

The Great War ended in November 1918, but it had taken its toll on Lakeland families. "Eleven men from the parish of Sawrey had lost their lives, and twenty-one from nearby Hawkshead." And Beatrix herself had faced another unexpected tragedy earlier that summer. Her beloved brother Bertram died of a cerebral hemorrhage at his home near Ancrum, Scotland, on June 22, 1918. He was only 46.

She wrote to her dear friend Hardwicke Rawnsley in September, "It is good to remember how much more cheerful & contented he had seemed towards the last. . . . He is buried . . . in a flowery graveyard with a ruined ivy grown church."

Then in 1919, Beatrix wrote to Millie Warne, "He had such a fine farm. His death was a great shock to us. He had been very subject to violent nose bleeding, and last spring it had not bled as it usually did, and then it was haemorhage [sic] on the brain. A merciful death, quite painless."

Beatrix and Bertram had rarely seen each other after he moved to Scotland, but they always shared a special bond—just as they'd shared a nursery, childhood adventures, painting, a love of natural history, animals, farming, and a desire to leave London to live in the countryside. He'd often written to Beatrix advising her on farming practices, and she looked forward to his visits, although they were infrequent. She was also grateful he'd shown the courage to stand up to their parents when she wanted to marry William.

Bertram had indeed battled "it" (alcoholism), as well as frequent bouts of depression. He was sensitive yet very talented and artistic. It had been hard having Bertram so far away, but Beatrix was glad that he'd found happiness with Mary; that comforted her. She and Mary had a good relationship, and Beatrix visited her sister-in-law often in the years to come. But the ache of losing her younger brother remained for the rest of her life.

8

VENTURES AND
INVESTMENTS

---

*"[S]urely it is a blessing when old age is coming, to be
able still to understand and share the joy of life that is
being lived by the young."* —BEATRIX POTTER, *in a
letter to Nora Burt, June 5, 1931*

After the war, Beatrix and William returned to their
regular daily routines. He carried on with his work
as a solicitor and she as a farmer and occasional illustrator. They also enjoyed taking out their boat on Moss
Eccles Tarn in the late afternoon—William fished, and
Beatrix often sketched.

The ebb and flow of country and village life remained
the same as it had for centuries, although it was now

common to see modern farm machinery in the fields, wider roads to accommodate automobiles and tourists, and telephones, indoor plumbing, and electricity in many homes.

Beatrix, however, refused to have electricity installed at either Castle Cottage or Hill Top, although she did have it in her barns—she thought "the cows might like it!" She wrote by candlelight and lit the gas lamps only when William got home—"there were no exceptions—and housekeepers who objected did not remain long at Castle Cottage."

Beatrix had mixed feelings about automobiles, but she also realized how helpful they could be. They were also there to stay, so she might as well accept that fact and move forward with the times. By 1922, she and William owned two cars. Beatrix never learned to drive, thinking she was too old to learn, so she either rode with William or asked a farmhand to drive her where she wanted to go.

Another change occurred when the aging John Cannon retired, and he and his wife left Hill Top in the spring of 1919. The Cannons had been a big part of Beatrix's life since she'd first come to Near Sawrey, and Beatrix was sorry to see them go. She hired a new farm manager, John Mackereth, to take Cannon's place.

Beatrix had begun expanding her herd of black-and-white Belted Galloway cattle, and Mackereth knew a lot about the breed. She also wanted to continue breeding and growing her herd of Herdwick sheep, those "hard . . .

pretty-faced mountain sheep," so it was important to have "an honest, hard-working" farm manager to help her.

Unfortunately, it was also during 1918–1919 that both an outbreak of measles and the deadly worldwide influenza pandemic hit Near Sawrey. Beatrix was very concerned about the lack of good rural healthcare, especially for children and the elderly. She decided the village needed a highly trained district nurse to make home visits.

With her usual determination, Beatrix reached out to community leaders and another concerned neighbor and friend, Emily Fowkes, to see what could be done. By 1919, she'd helped set up a nursing trust in the area to support a district nurse who would serve Near Sawrey and other nearby villages until the National Health Service took over nearly 30 years later.

Beatrix also became involved in the Girl Guides organization, which is comparable to America's Girl Scouts. She'd missed having friends when she was a child and admired an organization that provided the opportunity for friendship and for doing something useful. She wrote to a friend that she wished Girl Guides had been "invented when she was young . . . it is a grand thing to enjoy play and enjoy work, which is what the Scouts & Guides learn to do."

Beatrix allowed the local Girl Guides troops to camp out on her land, gave autographed copies of her books

Beatrix often let Girl Guides camp on her land. The Girl Guides organization was also active in Canada. This photo shows Canadian Girl Guides on a camping trip in 1913. *Girl Guides of Canada from Canada / CC BY (https://creativecommons.org/licenses/by/2.0)*

as prizes for competitions, and cheered them on in their activities. She even encouraged some of them to pursue careers in nursing. Beatrix found pleasure in these friendships and was always delighted when any of the girls came back to visit her.

In addition, Beatrix became an advocate for the Invalid Children's Aid Association (ICAA), a national charity in England. She allowed the organization to use her Peter Rabbit design on a penny stamp collecting card and later a Christmas card the ICAA sold to raise money for various needs, including the purchase of a children's hospital bed. Beatrix had suffered many illnesses as a child and had a special desire to help others. However, she didn't like to call attention to her good deeds and always tried to avoid publicity.

Beatrix had known Miss Rebekah Owen, a wealthy, elegant American woman who lived in the nearby village of Hawkshead, since she bought Hill Top. She admired Miss Owen's taste in silver, books, and furniture, as well as her knowledge of literature, and they also shared a love of gardening and art. In fact, Beatrix wrote to Fruing Warne that Miss Owen had "proved to us that Americans can be 'educated & literary.'" In short, Beatrix had a high opinion of Americans.

Therefore, when she received a letter from Anne Carroll Moore, the superintendent of children's work with the New York Public Library, in the summer of 1921 asking if she could drop by the Heelis's home for a short visit, Beatrix agreed. Miss Moore was staying in nearby Grasmere after returning from France where she'd visited libraries devastated by the war and contributed picture books so they could reopen. She wanted to tell Beatrix more about her work.

Beatrix invited the librarian to lunch, and the two women hit it off immediately. It was refreshing to talk to another person about books, art, and current creative projects, and the visit was a huge success. Beatrix took her new friend on a tour of Hill Top Farm, then invited her to stay overnight at Castle Cottage with her and William.

Miss Moore had also brought her wooden doll, Nicholas Knickerbocker, which she featured in her own books, and Beatrix was enchanted. In fact, in Anne Carroll Moore recounted Nicholas's visit with Beatrix Potter in one chapter of her 1932 fictional children's book *Nicholas and the Golden Goose*.

Fruing had been wanting a sequel to *Appley Dapply* for years, but due to her failing eyesight and constant farmwork, Beatrix had not made much progress. Now, after Miss Moore's visit, Beatrix was inspired to continue working on the new book, *Cecily Parsley's Nursery Rhymes*. It was completed and ready for the 1922 Christmas season.

Over the years, Beatrix welcomed many American visitors to tea at Castle Cottage. According to biographer Linda Lear, "They all loved books, had an appreciation of children's literature and illustration, and all had well-mannered, interesting children who were delighted to see where Peter Rabbit lived."

Through her correspondence with Bertha Mahony, a friend of Anne Carroll Moore and one of the cofounders of the *Horn Book Magazine*, a Boston publication devoted to children and reading, Beatrix agreed to submit her biographical information for a reference book on children's authors in 1925. This proved to be a good move on Beatrix's part, as it introduced her and her work to more Americans.

A portion of Beatrix's submitted entry reflects exactly how she now identified herself: "Beatrix Potter is Mrs. William Heelis. She lives in the north of England, her home is among the mountains and lakes that she has drawn in her picture books. Her husband is a lawyer." She didn't think any other information than that was necessary!

Regardless, Beatrix would also go on to publish *The Fairy Caravan* in 1929, solely for her American audience. Her publisher was Alexander McKay. Ironically, she never wanted an English edition of the book because she felt the stories were "too personal—too autobiographical" to publish in her own country.

Soon after *The Fairy Caravan* was released, McKay began asking for another book. Because Beatrix knew Warne had been disappointed that *The Fairy Caravan* had only been released in America, she decided to offer her new book, *The Tale of Little Pig Robinson*, to both publishers in 1930. It would be the last of Beatrix's books in the Peter Rabbit series, but she would go on to write two more stories that were published only in America.

Sister Anne (1932) was a retelling of Bluebeard, the classic fairy tale about a murderous husband told from the perspective of his eighth wife's sister, Anne. It was the last book published during Beatrix's lifetime. *Wag-by-Wall*, a story about an old woman, her kettle, and her clock, was published in 1944, the year after Beatrix died. It was released first in the *Horn Book Magazine* and later in book form.

Beatrix wrote to Miss Mahony years later and humbly compared her work to the "wonderful, purposeful life of achievement" of their friend Anne Carroll Moore, stating, "I have just made stories to please myself because I never grew up!"

Hardwicke Rawnsley passed away on May 28, 1920. Beatrix had always supported his work with the National Trust, and his activism to protect the Lake District from overdevelopment by industries and railroads. He was passionate about maintaining the beautiful landscape and ensuring the public footpaths were kept open to the public. Rawnsley was also serious about preserving the region's culture and identity—and of course, promoting the reestablishment of fell farming and Herdwick sheep.

Beatrix had collaborated with Rawnsley on many occasions, but after his death she became even more committed to the cause. She was especially concerned about keeping the farms on the fells from being destroyed through commercial development. Therefore, when Troutbeck Park Farm became available for sale in 1923, Beatrix was the buyer. Troutbeck was (and still is) a beautiful property of almost 2,000 acres, large enough to support several thousand sheep.

Developers were getting ready to buy the rundown property and build vacation houses on the bottom land, but with William's knowledge and help, Beatrix was able to outbid them. Her intention was to rebuild the large high-fell farm and ultimately give it to the National Trust when she died. She and William gradually bought surrounding land and important road frontages, making it all but impossible for anyone to develop other property in the area. It was a brilliant plan that worked perfectly.

So began the huge effort to improve and reestablish Troutbeck Park Farm. A "large and important flock of Herdwick sheep" came with the property, and Beatrix intended to start her improvements with them. She hired Tom Storey, an expert shepherd, to manage the farm and flock. When she asked him what his wage should be, she doubled it. Thus began the lifelong, yet sometimes contentious, friendship, between the eccentric lady farmer and the loyal shepherd.

Beatrix had made a good choice. Storey and another shepherd named Joseph Moscrop, who was also special to Beatrix, went to work. And when John Mackereth, her Hill Top Farm manager, retired in 1927, Beatrix asked Storey to take his place. Eventually, Tom's brother-in-law, George Walker, became "head man" at Troutbeck Farm. Although Beatrix was very hands-on and liked to stay involved in the day-to-day decisions, Walker and his wife Lucy became invaluable employees, helping to transform the property into a prosperous working farm.

As her stake in Herdwick sheep farming increased, Beatrix made another move. She became one of the first female members of the Herdwick Sheep Breeders Association and is credited as having a huge influence in their preservation in the Lake District. She learned everything she could about these "loveable, silly sheep" and soon became an expert on the breed.

Beatrix also entered her sheep into shows, and according to a reminiscence by Tom Story, "We won prizes for Herdwicks that very first year at Hawkshead Show

Shepherd with sheep on a chilly morning. Circa 1880–1890. *Library of Congress Prints and Photographs Division, LC-USZ62-106148*

and she was as pleased as a dog with two tails. I went to every show with Mrs. Heelis. We were unbeaten with ewes from 1930 until 1939. She won all sorts of prizes, like silver teapots and salvers, and tankards—she used to give me the tankards. We got on well and I stayed for twenty years, but then I knew her. If you met Mrs. Heelis with her head down you just walked past. If she had her head up you said, 'Good morning.'"

Sheep breeders and showmen who didn't know Beatrix often underestimated her. Some believed that the "eccentric farmer in her dowdy Herdwick wool suit and wooden clogs" was a "sentimental old woman who loved sheep but did not know much about them." In reality, Beatrix was so knowledgeable about Herdwicks that she became a show judge of the sheep—and of sheepdogs. Moreover, in 1943, she became the first woman to be voted president-elect of the Herdwick Sheep Breeders Association but was unable to take office before she passed away.

Almost all of Beatrix's time had been taken up with her farmwork, sheep breeding, and renovation at Troutbeck Park Farm. She did manage to create *Jemima Puddle-Duck's Painting Book* in 1925, and there was a re-release of *The Roly-Poly Pudding*, renamed *The Tale of Samuel Whiskers*, in 1926. In the spring of 1927, she had also begun work on a *Peter Rabbit Almanac for 1929*, put together with odds and ends, but she did not like the process or the resulting book. When she received the last proofs to review, she wrote to Fruing, "Please let me know if this wretched sample is *final*? I know one thing; it is the first, and the last."

Sadly, Fruing didn't live to see the finished book himself. He died from a heart attack in February 1928 at the age of 66. After 30 years of working with him, Beatrix felt the loss deeply. Fruing was the last of the Warne sons to work for the company, so it was the end of an era. Fruing's brother-in-law, Arthur Stephens, took over as managing director at the firm, and for Beatrix it was like beginning all over again.

It's true that Beatrix may have been tired of working on books, but she wasn't above using her artwork to help a good cause. While working on the *Peter Rabbit Almanac* in 1927, she was also creating a series of full-color animal paintings to sell for one guinea each. The reason? She was trying to help save an endangered and historic strip of land near the Windermere ferry, called Cockshott Point, from town development. It was a lovely spot with a "peaceful view of the high fells across the lake," but the National Trust had not raised quite enough money to buy it.

Beatrix had an idea. She would ask her American readers if they would like to contribute to "The Windermere Fund" in exchange for one of her drawings. She had 50 original autographed drawings copied from four of her Peter Rabbit illustrations, which she mailed to Bertha

Mahony, editor of the *Horn Book Magazine*. She hoped her friend would act as a go-between and publish the appeal made by "Beatrix Potter and Peter Rabbit" and sponsored by the National Trust in an upcoming issue.

Miss Mahony was happy to help, and she published the endorsement in the August 1927 issue. Then she

The Lake Windermere steam ferry, English Lake District, between 1890 and 1900. Cockshott Point was near the ferry landing. *Library of Congress Prints and Photographs Division, LC-DIG-ppmsc-08534*

displayed the drawings in the window of the Bookshop for Boys & Girls in Boston (one of the first children's bookstores in America) for five dollars each. The venture was wildly successful, as customers lined up to pay for an original Potter drawing and help save the small strip of endangered English land.

By November, Beatrix reported to her American friends that the land had been safely purchased and thanked them for helping. She was especially grateful to Bertha Mahony (later Miller) for using her influence to make a difference.

Beatrix had often looked from Hill Top Farm toward the fells where her great-grandfather Abraham Crompton once owned land, probably feeling a connection to her past. That land was now part of the Monk Coniston Estate, an area of 4,000 acres, and included several farms and important Lakeland beauty spots. It came up for sale in 1940, and although the National Trust wanted to buy it and save it from development, the money wasn't available. Beatrix again stepped in to help. She was worried that if one person didn't buy the whole estate, it would be broken up—so she bought it herself. Then she offered to sell half of it to the National Trust at the price she'd paid as soon as it raised the money. She also said the National Trust would get the rest when she died, in remembrance of her great-grandfather.

Of course, the National Trust was interested. It raised the money and then asked Beatrix to manage the entire estate until someone else could take over, which she did for six years. With the purchase of the Monk Coniston Estate, Beatrix became one of the largest landowners in the area, and she was already one of the biggest donors to the National Trust. She had believed in Hardwicke Rawnsley's vision to preserve the Lake District, and now she was doing her best to make it a reality.

View from Hill Top Farm. *Image used by permission of author*

9

LAST YEARS
AND LEGACY

"I lift my eyes to the hills, and I am content to look at them from below." —BEATRIX POTTER, *in a letter to Samuel Cunningham*

Near Sawrey residents were used to seeing Beatrix, her little round, stooped figure wearing a suit made of Herdwick wool, clogs, a wool scarf around her neck, and a "brown felt hat clamped to her head with a black elastic under her chin," bustling around the village. Although she was getting older, her intense blue eyes still sparkled and her cheeks remained rosy. She also always carried her large black umbrella.

Beatrix never fussed much with her appearance, often drawing back her unruly gray hair into a careless bun.

Unfortunately, the rheumatic fever she'd had early in her life caused a "bare patch on the top of her head." She once half-joked with a friend that she briefly considered her father's old barrister's wig, stuck away in a box, but then remembered it had "little tails." When not wearing either her brown felt hat or trademark trilby, with its narrow brim angled down at the front and slightly turned up in the back, she put a lace cap on her head to hide her lack of hair.

Helen disapproved of her daughter's "unstylish countrywoman appearance." Unsurprisingly, the two still didn't get along, and Beatrix was often exasperated with her mother, who lived a life of ease, enjoying her canaries and her little dog, and doing needlework. Helen pretty much depended on her staff and her daughter to do everything for her, and Beatrix had handled the sale of the London house in 1924, the packing and moving of furniture and household items, and even Bertram's estate. Yet, Helen didn't approve of anything Beatrix did—including sheep farming or her work with the National Trust. On the other hand, Beatrix was frustrated that her mother, who had great wealth, would not consider making even a small contribution to the National Trust.

Moreover, Helen seemed to be in good health, while Beatrix continually suffered with bronchitis, colds, and other illnesses. Beatrix wrote to her cousin in 1930, "My mother is 91 and very well. I wish I were as little troubled as she is. If she gets a cold it is only a sniff—and I have been in bed twice this winter already. . . . She is very lucky in having good lungs, no rheumatism, and good eyesight."

Two years later, on December 20, 1932, however, Helen Leech Potter passed away from natural causes at the age of 93 and was buried beside her husband. Sixty-six-year-old Beatrix inherited everything from her mother's estate, making her an even wealthier woman. It's difficult to guess at Beatrix's emotions over losing her mother, her last immediate family member, but all ties to her old life were now gone. In a letter to Hardwicke Rawnsley's second wife, Nellie, she wrote, "My mother's long life was a link with times that are passed away, though still vivid in our memory."

Beatrix had never let negative feelings prevent her from being respectful or taking care of her parents, but she did not allow her mother to force her into a lifestyle she didn't want.

As biographer Linda Lear stated, "[Beatrix] intended to be as different from her mother as it was possible to be, and she intended to end her days being active, useful, and, if she were especially fortunate, out and about in the countryside she loved."

Beatrix carried on with her daily activities and even became enchanted with a new breed of dog, the Pekingese. She noted the dogs were "very [much] like a guinea pig or a Teddy bear with a tail"—and they made good "foot warmers." She found her "two little Pekingese ladies, Chuleh and Tzusee," to be very pleasant company in her advancing years, as she was now approaching her 70s.

She wrote to her cousin Caroline in early 1934, "I am still stiff, always over busy, & feeling old." She did complete a bit of writing, fulfilling her contracts with her American publisher. Most of her time, however, was

Yew Tree Farm, Coniston, England. *"Yew Tree Farm" by Odd Welles is licensed under CC BY-NC-ND 2.0*

spent doing the things she cared most about—conservation and preservation, tending her sheep, farming, and now restoring the farmhouse at Yew Tree Farm, which was part of the Monk Coniston Estate.

Yew Tree Farm is still one of the most photographed properties in the Lake District, and it was already attracting tourists in the 1930s. The farm was named for the famous yew tree that once stood on the land, and Beatrix thought the "typical north country farm-house, very well worth preserving." There was also a spinning gallery for wool that "ran across the front of the barn," which made Yew Tree Farm well known in the district.

Beatrix loved oak and mahogany furniture and excellent craftsmanship, and she wanted the house to have an artistic, homey look. She had no problem spending all the money that was necessary to get the property and farmhouse back into tip-top shape. Ultimately, to help offset some of the costs of restoration, Beatrix "turned the parlour of the farmhouse into a tearoom for tourists and walkers" in the summer of 1933. She wanted the public to understand the value of these old fell farms and farmhouses and realized that she could combine both preservation and education, while turning a profit.

Through the mid-1930s, both Beatrix and William experienced poor health and sickness. Beatrix continued to suffer from a weak heart and frequent bronchitis, but

Beatrix and Walt Disney

In 1936, Walt Disney tried to make a deal with Beatrix. He wanted to create an animated movie based on *The Tale of Peter Rabbit*, but she turned him down, stating that she felt her illustrations were not detailed enough to be magnified on a big screen. However, according to journalist Rebecca Mead in a 2018 article in the *New Yorker*, this could've simply been Beatrix's canny way of holding on to all of her copyrights.

in 1939, she was hospitalized for treatment of a serious condition and later, a dangerous surgery.

Initially, Beatrix had been concerned she might not survive her surgery, so she got all her affairs in order before she went to the hospital. One of the first things she did was to update her will so that all the copyrights of her work would go to William, and then to Norman Warne's favorite nephew, Frederick Warne Stephens, after William's death. They would later go to the publishing company when Frederick passed away.

Beatrix also began making Hill Top into a museum of sorts, arranging all of her personal and family items, treasures, and relics in the exact way she wanted them to be displayed after her death, just in case she didn't come back after the surgery. She already planned to leave the Hill Top property and house to the National Trust, so this task weighed heavy on her mind.

Her first biographer, Margaret Lane, wrote: "As she had kept it [Hill Top farmhouse] for more than forty years, so she wished it to remain; unchanged; not lived in by other people. She knew exactly how she wanted the china always in the cupboards, and where her great-grandfather's Bible and *Gerard's Herbal* and a particular candlestick were to stand for ever: and lay propped in bed with pencil and paper, writing minute directions. She could not lie easy until her mind had dwelt in peace on that inner vision." In fitting fashion, Beatrix even turned the family Bible to Psalm 23, beginning with the verse, "The Lord is my Shepherd . . ." It is still displayed today just as she left it all those years ago.

Thankfully, Beatrix's operation was successful, although there were complications, and she had a long recovery. But there were other worries as well. The rumblings of another war had been heard for years, but it became a reality when Adolph Hitler and his German army invaded Poland on September 1, 1939. Both France and the United Kingdom declared war on Germany, and thus World War II began. Life was again turned upside down with the resulting fear of air raids and bombing, food shortages, a lack of farm help, and trying to produce farm goods and wool for military use.

The village of Near Sawrey escaped damage from German bombers, but Beatrix's childhood home at

This Beatrix Potter Society blue plaque marks the site where Beatrix Potter used to live. The plaque is attached to a wall on the southeast side of Old Brompton Road. The Bousfield Primary School was built on this location in 1954. *Image used by permission of author*

2 Bolton Gardens did not. Word came from London that the house had been destroyed by a bomb on October 10, 1940. Beatrix did not mourn its loss, calling it her "unloved birthplace" and proclaiming that she was "rather pleased to hear it is no more!"

As the years of the war progressed, Beatrix took comfort in writing letters to both old and new friends in England and in America. She also continued her involvement in the Girl Guides organization and was surprised when the girls hosted an impromptu party to celebrate her 75th birthday in 1941 and dressed up as the characters from her little books. As each girl stepped forward to greet her, Beatrix had to guess who they were.

Toward the end of 1943, Beatrix began to weaken. She had caught a cold, then developed bronchitis—and her damaged heart could not keep up. She wrote Christmas letters to friends in November, but she knew she didn't have long to live. In a letter to her cousin Caroline, she spoke of the fells and beautiful countryside she would never see again. As she had done as a child, she could not bear to think of a place too altered from the way she remembered it, preferring to picture it in her mind as it had been, rather than how it might have changed. She wrote, "It is some years ago since I have walked on the beloved hills, but I remember every stone & rock—and *stick*. I think it is pleasanter to remember an old stunted thorn or holly than to go to the spot and find it gone."

Next, Beatrix charged her shepherd, friend, and farm manager, Tom Storey, with an important job. She told him that after her death, she was to be cremated. She wanted him to scatter her ashes above Hill Top in the place where she'd often walked and sketched, but she wanted the location to be kept secret.

Helen Beatrix Potter Heelis died at Castle Cottage on Wednesday, December 22, 1943, at the age of 77. William was by her side at death, just as he'd been in life, forever faithful yet desperately heartbroken. Beatrix

Beatrix placed her personal items in the Hill Top farmhouse the way she wanted them displayed. Visitors can see her hat and gloves on chairs and her clogs underneath. *Image used by permission of author*

departed the world quietly and without fuss—just as she would've wanted.

Tom Storey and William scattered Beatrix's ashes in the exact spot she had specified. When William died 18 months later, in August 1945, Storey scattered his ashes in the same place, ensuring the two were together again.

The loyal shepherd followed Beatrix's last request and
kept the spot a secret until he lay on his own deathbed in
1986 at the age of 90. Only then did he confide the location to his son. When Tom Storey's son died unexpect-
edly several years later, the "secret properly passed to
the ages."

As biographer Linda Lear noted, "It is enough to
know only that Beatrix returned to her beloved hills."

Beatrix's legacy was great. Of course, the royalties and
rights to her books went to Frederick Stephens after William died, but everything else was left to the National
Trust, including 15 farms (with numerous farmhouses,
outbuildings, and cottages), 4,000 acres of land, and the
rest of her manuscripts, illustrations, and drawings.

William also carried out Beatrix's wish that Hill
Top be preserved by the National Trust as a permanent
memorial, and so it remains to this day. Thousands of
people from all over the world visit Beatrix's farmhouse
and garden each year, and it's easy to feel as though one
has stepped back in time and the author herself will be
returning from one of her errands in the village at any
moment.

Beatrix was ahead of her time in many ways. As a
young, unmarried woman in the Victorian era, she
initially forged her own creative path to independence,
fame, and financial success. She was indeed a talented

Mrs. Who?

Margaret Lane, Beatrix's first biographer, had an interesting take on the author's death. In a tribute published in an early 1944 issue of *Housewife Magazine*, Lane asserted that quite a few Lakeland residents were surprised to learn that Mrs. William Heelis of Near Sawrey was the Beatrix Potter of Peter Rabbit fame—and that she had been living in the area for years. Many people figured she'd passed away long before 1943! Mrs. Lane fancied that Beatrix would not have been offended at all.

"Her extreme reserve, the passionate care with which she concealed herself from the public, the almost obsessional precautions which she took against celebrity, had succeeded so well that the world obligingly assumed that she was dead. Revealed at last, however, by the publicity of death, she emerges as one always hoped she would— short, solid, apple-cheeked, in flower-trimmed hat and shapeless garment, full of character and a particular delicate understating sort of humour, not without its touch of acerbity. She was, we find, a country body looking not altogether unlike Mrs. Tiggy-Winkle; a woman who had lived all her life

(continued on next page)

(continued from previous page)

in the Lake District and was in love with it; who, out of her feeling for its woods and dales as she remembered them in childhood, its stone-floored farmhouses and cottage gardens profuse with snapdragons and tiger lilies, and out of her own imaginative observation, amounting to genius, of its farmyard and hedgerow animals, created a tiny world of pure and satisfying fantasy."

author and illustrator, giving the world her "little books" that have been enjoyed by children for well over a century. But she was so much more than the creator of watercolor bunnies wearing little blue jackets or naïve ducks waddling about in bonnets and shawls. She was a trailblazer in the areas of natural science, mycology, animal science, conservation, and preservation. She was a savvy businesswoman, sometimes impatient and curt, who never backed down from a challenge. Yet, she was forever content to simply be known as Mrs. Heelis, wife, village resident, farmer, and sheep breeder.

Beatrix was also a visionary and an exceptional steward of the land. She championed the preservation and reintroduction of Herdwick sheep in the area. In fact, she even left strict instructions about maintaining the numbers of pure Herdwicks on some of [her] properties.

And thanks to her efforts to save and protect the endangered fells and valleys of the Lake District, countless generations will enjoy the beautiful, unchanged landscapes and vistas that she loved so well.

Beatrix Portrayed and Celebrated

Beatrix's life and her work and characters have been portrayed and celebrated in biographies, documentaries, full-length movie dramas, animated films, plays, and themed attraction venues. There are dedicated Beatrix Potter YouTube channels and Instagram accounts, exhibitions, and ballets, and special commemorative coins were released to celebrate her 150th birthday in 2016. There is also at least one English primary school named in her honor.

In addition to her Hill Top Farm home in Near Sawrey, there is also a Beatrix Potter Gallery and Museum in William's former law office in nearby Hawkshead. This 17th-century building houses a large collection of Beatrix's art, original dummy manuscripts, letters, and more. Moreover, the Armitt Museum in Ambleside holds many of her botanical and fungi watercolors, quite a few of her

(continued on next page)

(continued from previous page)

family's books, and several first editions of her little tales. The Victoria and Albert Museum in London also houses a very large collection of Beatrix Potter's original manuscripts, books, illustrations, family items, and artifacts. The museum's organizers frequently create special exhibitions to showcase and highlight Beatrix Potter's work and life.

Visitors to the English Lake District will also find Yew Tree Farm, Tarn Hows, Lake Windermere, Wray Castle, the World of Peter Rabbit, and filming locations from the movie *Miss Potter* to be of great interest. Indeed, Beatrix Potter fans will find much to enjoy and explore around and about the beautiful Cumbrian villages and scenic landscapes.

Beatrix Potter enthusiasts may also be interested in joining the Beatrix Potter Society, a registered charitable organization established in the United Kingdom in 1980 to promote the study and appreciation of the life and works of Beatrix Potter. Membership is open worldwide, and the group hosts yearly meetings, sponsors special events and projects, prints and mails/e-mails materials and newsletters to members, and provides a platform for Beatrix Potter fans to connect with each other, no matter where they live.

ACKNOWLEDGMENTS

Creating a book is never a solitary endeavor—and I've had a lot of help along the way. First, thanks to CRP senior editor, Jerry Pohlen, and assistant project editor, Frances Giguette, for their patience, guidance, and expertise as we've worked together to make this book the very best it can be. And a big shout-out to everyone else at Chicago Review Press and Independent Publishers Group as well.

Thanks to Annemarie Bilclough (also a Beatrix Potter Society member) and Lucy Shaw at the Victoria and Albert Museum in London, who provided invaluable help during my research phase and the subsequent visit to the Blythe House in early 2020, and to Freya Levett, V&A image-licensing expert, for her assistance. I also appreciate the members of the Beatrix Potter Society, who were always ready to assist with information, photo research, image procurement—and encouragement. I'd especially like to thank BPS members Kathy Cole, Suzanne Terry, and Libby Joy for their help, support, and interest.

I would like to thank and honor "Miss" Lois Fletcher, my very first teacher at Irwin Academy and local educational legend. Miss Lois invested her time and love into countless preschool children over the years, and I remember all the wonderful picture books and stories she shared. It's true that I had to sit in her time-out "sugar chair" occasionally, but I know beyond a doubt that this sweet lady helped instill in me a love of reading and books—and eventually the desire to create my own stories.

I couldn't do what I do without my whole family! I appreciate the unwavering support of my parents, Edward and Betty McIntyre, my sister, Mindy McHugh, my in-loves Roger and Peggy O'Quinn, and the rest of the crew on both sides. And, as always, a great big thank you to my husband, Chad, and our children, Erin, Elisabeth, Wesley, Morgan, Ellie, John, and Alexander. I love and appreciate you all!

Notes

After the first reference, JBP refers to The Journal of Beatrix Potter, *followed by the date of her entry.*

1: BEGINNINGS AT 2 BOLTON GARDENS

"My brother and I": Jane Crowell Morse (ed.), *Beatrix Potter's Americans: Selected Letters* (Boston: The Horn Book, 1982), 213.

"obstinate, hard headed": Morse, 207.

"I can remember quite plainly": Morse, 208.

"the place I love best": Potter, Beatrix, *The Journal of Beatrix Potter, from 1881 to 1897,* Transcribed from her code writing by Leslie Linder (London: Frederick Warne & Co., 1966), 1891.

"the sweet balmy air": JBP, 1891.

"the notes of the stable clock": JBP, 1891.

"There was something rapturous": JBP, 1891.

"Everything was romantic": JBP, Thursday, May 8, 1884.

"So it sometimes happens": Margaret Lane, *The Tale of Beatrix Potter: A Biography* (London and New York: Frederick Warne & Co., 1946), 20.

"home to her heart": Linda Lear, *Beatrix Potter: A Life in Nature* (New York: St. Martin's Press, 2007), 27.

"liked [to hear]" and *"goody goody"*: Judy Taylor, *Beatrix Potter: Artist, Storyteller, and Countrywoman* (Harmondsworth, Middlesex, England: Frederick Warne & Co. and Penguin Books, 1986), 20.

"Of course, what I wore": Morse, 208.

"mine used to be": Morse, 59.

2: GIRLHOOD AND GROWING UP

"I do not remember": Morse, 147.

"Hoisted on to the top": JBP, July 26, 1892.

"The difficulty was to": JBP, July 26, 1892.

"Sally (the snake)": JBP, September 21, 1883.

"freehand, model, geometry": JBP, May 28, 1883.

"Painting is an awkward": JBP, May 28, 1883.

"Of course, I shall paint": JBP, November 21, 1883.

"It is all the same": JBP, October 4, 1884.

"I felt fit to kick": JBP, June 21, 1883.

"in the middle of September": JBP, October 4, 1884.

"plenty of people": JBP, August 13, 1896.

"I never thought there": JBP, January 13, 1883.

"I had rather a picture": JBP, March 15, 1885.

"took particular note": Lear, 48.

"I will do something": JBP, March 3, 1883.

"I used to write": Lear, 49.

"probably stopped by": JBP, May 11, 1882.

"Went to Hawkshead": JBP, August 19, 1882.

"man of high confidence": Lear, 53.

"introduced her to his conviction": Taylor (1986), 39.

"someone who loved": Taylor (1986), 39.

3: FEVERS AND FUNGI

"Now of all hopeless": JBP, October 29, 1892.

"cutting off more and more": JBP, April 25, 1883.

"I thought to have": JBP, April 25, 1883.

"Dear old man": JBP, June 12, 1884.

"a great deal of pleasure": JBP, April 20, 1884.

"happy and affectionate" and "sweetest animal": JBP, December 1886.

"I wish for many things": JBP, December 13, 1884.

"I feel an extraordinary dislike": JBP, May 8, 1884.

"the future is dark": JBP, May 8, 1884.

"I am eighteen today": JBP, July 28, 1884.

"the responsibility of": JBP, September 16, 1884.

"I wonder how he": JBP, June 28, 1884.

"Now that the sheep": JBP, March 28, 1884.

"very good-natured": JBP, July 10, 1885.

"If this is what beauty": JBP, September 7, 1885.

"terribly afraid of the future": JBP, December 31, 1885.

"could not be turned": JBP, 1887.

"Amazed to find myself": JBP, 1887.

"Such drawings suggest": Lear, 71.

"that charming rascal": JBP, May 1890.

"she was very pretty": Leslie Linder, The History of the Tale of Peter Rabbit (London: Frederick Warne & Co., 1976), 10.

"I would not make fun": JBP, October 29, 1892.

4: DISCOVERIES, DISREGARD, AND THE ROAD TO RECOGNITION

"My dear Noel,": Linder (1976), 11.

"bought at a very tender age": Leslie Linder, *A History of the Writings of Beatrix Potter* (London: Frederick Warne & Co., 1971), 110.

"an affectionate companion": Linder (1971), 110.

"In the space of two days": Lear, 87.

"dislike of babies": JBP, 1894.

"Latter day fate": JBP, 1894.

"seemed to like her drawings": JBP, May 19, 1896.

"I think one of my pleasantest": JBP, September 21, 1896.

"On the Germination": JBP, January 31, 1897.

"My paper was read": Lear, 124.

"market her fanciful drawings": Lear, 130.

"[Miss Potter] would rather": Judy Taylor, *Letters to Children from Beatrix Potter* (London: Frederick Warne & Co., 1992), 66.

"modest sum of 1/2d": Linder (1976), 19.

"top billing in the list": Lear, 155.

"written to a child": Linder (1976), 10.

5: MORE LITTLE BOOKS, LOVE, AND LOSS

"I thought my story": Lear, 204.

"his tools and the snippets": Linder (1971), 112.

"the tale was a fairy story": Lear, 157.

"I bought two [squirrels]": Taylor (1986), 83.

"I am going to meet": Taylor (1986), 75.

"most beautiful 18th century clothing": Taylor (1986), 85.

"For the first time": Lear, 166.

"I had been a little hoping": Sarah Gristwood, *The Story of Beatrix Potter* (London: National Trust Books, 2016), 71.

"like to get some new work": Judy Taylor, *Beatrix Potter's Letters* (London: Frederick Warne & Co., 1989), 122.

"for her story to come out right": Lear, 171.

6: FROM LONDON TO THE LAKE DISTRICT

"I must try to make": Judy Taylor (ed.), *Beatrix Potter: A Holiday Diary* (London: Beatrix Potter Society, 1996), 58.

"My purchase seems to be": Taylor (1989), 133.

"sixteen ewes so there": Taylor (1986), 108.

"was not impressed with": Marta McDowell, *Beatrix Potter's Gardening Life* (Portland, OR: Timber Press, 2013), 12.

"I stole some 'honesty' yesterday": McDowell, 93.

"It will be a trying thing": Taylor (1989), 125.

"I know some people": Taylor (1989), 125.

"Beatrix Potter loved unusual words,": Linder (1971), 195.

"It is said that the effect,": Beatrix Potter, *The Tale of the Flopsy Bunnies* (London: Frederick Warne & Co., 1909), 9.

7: MRS. HEELIS

"there is a great deal of work": Taylor (1989), 264.

"made her realize": Lear, 259.

"William has actually been": Taylor (1989), 212.

"it [would] have to be": Taylor (1989), 214.

"collect a new white bull": Lear, 261.

"I am Mrs. Heelis now": Lear, 261.

"Beatrix began her new life": Lear, 265.

"My eyes are gone": Taylor (1989), 221.

"had little patience": Lear, 271.

"urged farmers not only": Lear, 272.

"[S]he is quite out of the common": Lear, 275.

"accused of passing £20,000 worth": Gristwood, 106.

"never meddles again": Taylor (1989), 247.

"Eleven men from the parish": Andrew Norman, *Beatrix Potter: Her Inner World* (Barnsley, South Yorkshire, England: Pen & Sword History, 2014), 147.

"It is good to remember": Taylor (1989), 251.

"He had such a fine farm": Blythe House Collection (London), Letter to Millie Warne from Beatrix Potter, November 8, 1919.

8: VENTURES AND INVESTMENTS

"[S]urely it is a blessing": Taylor (1989), 341.

"the cows might like it!": Gristwood, 130.

"there were no exceptions": Gristwood, 130.

"hard . . . pretty-faced": Lane, 138.

"an honest, hard-working": Lear, 302.

"invented when she was young": Lear, 309.

"proved to us that Americans": Taylor (1989), 269.

"They all loved books": Lear, 315.

"Beatrix Potter is": John Heelis, *The Tale of Mrs. William Heelis, Beatrix Potter* (Gloucestershire, England: Sutton Publishing, 2003), vii.

"too personal—too autobiographical": Linder (1971), 292.

"wonderful, purposeful life" and *"I have just made stories"*: Morse, 177.

"large and important flock": Lear, 321.

"loveable, silly sheep": Lane, 141.

"We won prizes": Taylor (1986), 163–164.

"eccentric farmer in her dowdy": Lear, 330.

"Please let me know": Taylor (1989), 305.

"peaceful view of the high fells": Lear, 338.

9: LAST YEARS AND LEGACY

"I lift my eyes": Lear, 430.

"brown felt hat": Lear, 334.

"bare patch" and *"little tails"*: Lear, 382.

"unstylish countrywoman appearance": Lear, 367.

"My mother is 91": Taylor (1989), 336.

"My mother's long life": Lane, 138.

"[Beatrix] intended to be": Lear, 369.

"very [much] like a guinea pig": Gristwood, 130.

"foot warmers": Lear, 385.

"two little Pekingese ladies": Lear, 385.

"I am still stiff": Taylor (1989), 361.

"typical north country": Lear, 374–375.

"turned the parlour of the farmhouse": Lear, 375.

"As she had kept it": Lane, 156.

"unloved birthplace": Lear, 421.

"rather pleased": Lear, 421.

"It is some years ago": Lear, 439.

"secret properly passed": Lear, 441.

"It is enough to know": Lear, 441.

"Her extreme reserve": Margaret Lane, "The Art of Beatrix Potter: A Tribute to the Most Delightful Writer of Children's Books," *The Housewife Magazine*, 1944. (This write-up was included in the Beatrix Potter Society newsletter, *Pottering About*—Beatrix Potter e-News, no. 76, December 2020.)

BIBLIOGRAPHY

Titles marked with an asterisk are especially appropriate for young readers.

Crouch, Marcus. *Beatrix Potter: A Walck Monograph.* New York: Henry Z. Walck, 1961.

Crow, Vivienne. *Beatrix Potter's Lake District: Cumbria.* Rotherham, England: National Trust, 2016.

Denyer, Susan. *At Home with Beatrix Potter: The Creator of Peter Rabbit.* London: Frances Lincoln Limited in Association with The National Trust (Enterprises), 2000.

*Fabiny, Sarah. *Who Was Beatrix Potter?* New York: Penguin Workshop, an imprint of Penguin Random House, 2015.

*Gristwood, Sarah. *The Story of Beatrix Potter.* London: National Trust Books, 2016.

*Hallinan, Camilla. *The Ultimate Peter Rabbit: A Visual Guide to the World of Beatrix Potter.* New York: DK Publishing, 2016.

Heelis, John. *The Tale of Mrs. William Heelis, Beatrix Potter.* Gloucestershire, England: Sutton Publishing, 2003.

*Johnson, Jane. *The True Story of Peter Rabbit: How a Letter from Beatrix Potter Became a Children's Classic.* New York: Puffin Books, 1999.

*Lane, Margaret. *The Tale of Beatrix Potter: A Biography.* London and New York: Frederick Warne & Co., 1946.

Lear, Linda. *Beatrix Potter: A Life in Nature.* New York: St. Martin's Press, 2007.

Linder, Leslie. *A History of the Writings of Beatrix Potter, Including Unpublished Work.* London: Frederick Warne & Co., 1971.

Linder, Leslie. *The History of The Tale of Peter Rabbit.* London: Frederick Warne & Co., 1976.

*Marshall, Linda. *Saving the Countryside: The Story of Beatrix Potter and Peter Rabbit.* Brooklyn, NY: little bee books., January 2020.

Marxer, Jordan. *Our Hearts Are in England.* Birmingham, AL: Hoffman Media, 83 Press, 2019.

Masset, Claire. *Beatrix Potter's Hill Top, Cumbria.* Rotherham, England: National Trust, 2016.

McDowell, Marta. *Beatrix Potter's Gardening Life, The Plants and Places That Inspired the Classic Children's Tales.* Portland, OR: Timber Press, 2013.

*Metcalf, Lindsay H. *Beatrix Potter, Scientist.* Park Ridge, Illinois: Albert Whitman & Co., September 2020.

Mitchell, W. R. *Beatrix Potter: Her Lakeland Years.* Ilkley, England: Great Northern Books, 2010.

Morse, Jane Crowell, ed. *Beatrix Potter's Americans: Selected Letters.* Boston: The Horn Book, 1982.

Norman, Andrew. *Beatrix Potter: Her Inner World.* Barnsley, South Yorkshire, England: Pen & Sword History, 2014.

Potter, Beatrix. *The Journal of Beatrix Potter, from 1881 to 1897.* Transcribed from her code writing by Leslie Linder. London: Frederick Warne & Co., 1966.

Taylor, Judy. *Beatrix Potter and Hawkshead, Cumbria.* London: National Trust, 1996.

Taylor, Judy, ed. *Beatrix Potter: A Holiday Diary, with a Short History of the Warne Family.* London: Beatrix Potter Society, 1996.

*Taylor, Judy. *Beatrix Potter: Artist, Storyteller, and Countrywoman.* Harmondsworth, Middlesex, England: Frederick Warne & Co. and Penguin Books, 1986.

Taylor, Judy. *Beatrix Potter's Letters.* London: Frederick Warne & Co., 1989.

Taylor, Judy. *Letters to Children from Beatrix Potter.* London: Frederick Warne & Co., 1992.

Wright, John D. *The Victorians: From Empire and Industry to Poverty and Famine.* London: Amber Books, 2018.

INDEX

Page numbers in italics *refer to pictures.*